Sweet Tea for the Soul

DOWN-HOME DEVOTIONS TO COMFORT THE HEART

Sweet Tea for the Soul: Down-Home Devotions to Comfort the Heart
Copyright © 2018 by DaySpring
Second Edition, March 2018

Published by:

DaySpring

P.O. Box 1010
Siloam Springs, AR 72761
dayspring.com

Bible verses were taken from the following translations:

AMP: Scriptures taken from the Amplified® Bible, © 1954, 1958, 1962, 1964, 1965, 1987 by The Lockman Foundation. Used by permission. (www.lockman.org)

ESV: Scripture quotations taken from the ESV Bible® (The Holy Bible, English Standard Version®) copyright ©2001 by Crossway Bibles, a publishing ministry of Good News Publishers. Used by permission. All rights reserved.

HCSB: Scripture taken from the Holman Christian Standard Bible®. © 1999, 2000, 2002, 2003 by Holman Bible Publishers. Used by permission.

KJV: Scripture taken from the Holy Bible, King James Version.

The Message: Scripture quotations from The Message. © Eugene Peterson. Permission from NavPress

NASB: Scripture from the NEW AMERICAN STANDARD BIBLE *, © Copyright 1960, 1962, 1963, 1968, 1971, 1972, 1973, 1975, 1977, 1995 by the Lockman Foundation. Used by permission. (www.lockman.org)

NIV: Scriptures marked NIV are taken from the Holy Bible, New International Version®, NIV®. Copyright © 1973, 1978, 1984, 2011 by Biblica, Inc.® Used by permission of Zondervan. All rights reserved worldwide. www.zondervan.com. The "NIV" and "New International Version" are trademarks registered in the United States Patent and Trademark Office by Biblica, Inc.®

NKJV: Scripture from the New King James Version. Copyright © 1982 by Thomas Nelson, Inc.

NLT: Scripture quotations are taken from the Holy Bible, New Living Translation, copyright © 1996, 2004, 2007 by Tyndale House Foundation. Used by permission of Tyndale House Publishers, Inc., Carol Stream, Illinois 60188. All rights reserved.

TLB: © The Living Bible. Taken from the Living Bible with permission from Tyndale House Publishers, Inc., Wheaton, IL.

Written by Linda Kozar
Designed by Jessica Wei
Typeset by Greg Jackson of thinkpen.design

Printed in China

Prime: 71932

ISBN: 978-1-68408-223-0

TABLE OF CONTENTS

A MESSAGE TO READERS

Because you've picked up a devotional book with the word "Sweet Tea" in its title, you probably have more than a passing interest in both old-time religion and down-home country wisdom. If so, you've come to the right place. On the pages that follow, you'll be treated to a collection of timely wisdom, timeless Scripture, inspirational quotes, and daily devotionals. And as you read along day by day, you'll discover a dash of down-home country humor, too.

In rural America, the Christian faith has been expressed for centuries through song and verse. Today, the gospel message remains near and dear to millions of believers who still enjoy the simple pleasures of a quiet evening spent talking and rocking on the front porch. The ideas in this book remind us that God's grace is free, that His love endures forever, and that His faithfulness extends to good ol' boys and city folk alike.

The Bible is a book like no other. It is a gift from the Creator, an instruction book for life here on Earth and a roadmap for life eternal. And it's a book of promises. When God makes a promise, He keeps it. No exceptions. So the verses in this text are not hypotheticals; they're certainties. They apply to every generation, to every nationality, and to every corner of the globe, including yours. And His promises apply to every human being, including you.

If you're ready for a heaping helping of inspiration and truth, keep reading. When you do, you'll discover that old-time religion has never gone out of style...and never will.

FELLOWSHIPPING FIREFLIES

Let your light so shine before men, that they may see
your good works and glorify your Father in heaven.
MATTHEW 5:16 NKJV

In the Great Smoky Mountains of Tennessee, during a two-week mating period in late spring, a unique species of fireflies is known to synchronize their flashing light patterns. Unlike other species of fireflies that blink their lights randomly, these bioluminescent beauties flicker their individual lights at the same time.

The Bible says that we are to walk as children of light (Ephesians 5:7–14) in a darkened world. The fruit of the light is found in goodness and righteousness and truth. When we live our lives in sync with God's Word, we shine with Him, the Light of the World (John 8:12), and we shine to His glory, piercing the darkness of this age.

FAITH CHECK

These special fireflies do not always flash in unison. Sometimes they flash in waves across the midnight hillsides. At other times, they flash together in harmonious short bursts that end in sudden periods of darkness. Sometimes our lives look a lot like that too. But when we set our hearts to love God and one another, we cannot fail to shine.

All I want to
do is sit on the
front porch
and watch
the fireflies.

GET YOUR GOAT

You shall not be afraid of the terror by night, nor of the arrow that flies by day, nor of the pestilence that walks in darkness, nor of the destruction that lays waste at noonday.

PSALM 91:5-6 NKJV

There is a certain breed of domestic goat that is known to faint when startled. At the sound of a loud noise, its hind leg muscles freeze up for about ten seconds and this "fainting goat" collapses on its side like a sack of potatoes!

What happens when the enemy catches *you* off guard? Are you temporarily paralyzed with fear? Many of us feel like keeling over when troubles suddenly come. We are overwhelmed by feelings of helplessness, anxiety, uncertainty, and fear. These are all natural responses, but faith is a supernatural response to these feelings. Believers have a choice—to freeze in fear or flex their faith muscles. Speak His Word over your circumstance. Proclaim the name of Jesus over your fear. Don't worry about what people think. Instead, open your Bible and find out what God has to say about the situation.

FAITH CHECK

We don't have to let fear floor us. Let's take our eyes off our circumstances and look to Christ instead. After all, faith is what separates the sheep from the goats.

If you don't want someone to get your goat, don't tell them where it's tied up.

THE PEARL

Coral and quartz are not worth mentioning. The price of wisdom is beyond pearls.

JOB 28:18 HCSB

A raw oyster is not much to look at on the outside, but enthusiastic fans of these saltwater mollusks find them delicious with the addition of a little hot sauce, horseradish, and lemon juice. Sometimes a raw oyster even contains an unexpected bonus: a pearl. Natural pearls form as a defense mechanism, an immune response from the little gray creature inside the shell against a potentially threatening irritant. The irritant is covered, layer by layer, with nacre, a mineral substance also known as mother-of-pearl. The very best pearls have a metallic sheen, a mirror-like luster from the many coatings swathed around the irritant. Beautiful luminescent layers smooth over the irritation to make life more comfortable for the little guys, and over time they form a highly sought after treasure from the depths of the waters.

FAITH CHECK

When someone irritates us, we should take a cue from the oyster and cover the person with our prayers. We should coat the rough, unlovable one with our forgiveness and the love of God. And in time, with enough love and patience, the one who irritated us may become a blessing and a comfort to us instead. A precious pearl, a thing of great beauty.

Pearls do
not lie on the
seashore. Those
who desire one
must dive for it.

CHINESE PROVERB

THE FINGER TRAP

God met me more than halfway, He freed me from my anxious fears.
PSALM 31:4 THE MESSAGE

Y**ou** most likely came into contact with one as a child: a small, colorful cylinder made of woven bamboo. Instructed by snickering friends to insert your index fingers into each end, you discovered to your dismay that your fingers were now trapped inside. The more you pulled outward, the tighter the aptly named Finger Trap became. After a good laugh your friends told you the secret of breaking free. Instead of pulling in the outward direction, you surrender to the inward direction. The taut cylinder then relaxes and the captive fingers are loosed. *Ta-da!*

FAITH CHECK

At times, most of us resort to running away from our problems. But rather than run, we should press in to God. In lieu of tensing up, we should relax and quit fighting so hard to break away in our own strength. We can make the impossible work to our advantage by trusting in the God of the impossible to help us.

Common sense
is a flower that
doesn't grow
in everyone's
garden.

THE BRASS RING

I have seen all the works that are done under the sun;
and indeed, all is vanity and grasping for the wind.
ECCLESIASTES 1:14 NKJV

No doubt you've seen them. Manes flying, nostrils flaring, wooden horses captured in colorful elegance gallop up and down on a carousel to the delight of children and adults. Traditional European merry-go-rounds turn clockwise, allowing proper equestrians to mount the ornately carved wooden horses from the left. However, Americans are less concerned with proper equestrian form than they are with the opportunity to acquire the much-sought-after brass ring. American carousels were designed in the nineteenth century to travel counter-clockwise, allowing riders to grab for the brass ring with their right hand. Any rider who could reach out and grab the ring was rewarded with a prize—a free ride on the carousel. In time, grabbing the brass ring became a metaphor for success and opportunity.

FAITH CHECK

True success comes from setting goals, learning from mistakes, and strong faith, perseverance, and honest hard work. Those who disdain these elements prefer to ride a carousel seeking worldly success and will grasp for it in vain on an endless circuit. Instead of reaching for a shiny brass ring, let's reach out to Jesus.

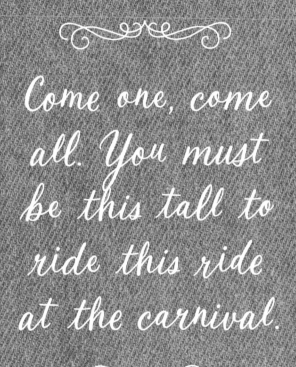

Come one, come all. You must be this tall to ride this ride at the carnival.

HARPS UPON THE WILLOWS

On the willow trees in the midst of Babylon we hung our harps.
PSALM 137:2 AMP

When the kingdom of Judah was taken captive and carried away to Babylon, there were among them many musicians who sought solace through their gifts, praising God near the abundant willow trees on the banks of the waters there. The Babylonians heard their sweet songs and bid the musicians entertain them. But rather than offer sacred songs to men, they hung their harps upon the willows, considering it far better to put their instruments aside than to profane them in the service of idols. The willow branches seemed to weep, drooping under the weight of the harps, much as the hearts of these faithful worshippers. They could have dashed their harps to pieces, but instead they preserved their instruments, because God told them through the prophet Jeremiah precisely when their time of captivity would end (Jeremiah 29:10).

FAITH CHECK

What should you do when faced with a choice like that? Whether you find yourself facing persecutions, trials, or temptations, you may have to make a similar commitment to honor God by laying your harp upon the willows.

Knowing we will be with Christ forever far outweighs our burdens today! Keep your eyes on eternity.

BILLY GRAHAM

THEY THAT MOURN

A time to weep and a time to laugh;
a time to mourn and a time to dance.
ECCLESIASTES 3:4 NIV

In the old South, mourning used to be a big deal. No decent Southerner would be sent to the hereafter without a lengthy ceremony and an even more extended period of mourning. Women wore black hats and dresses, swishing the sweltering air with hand-held funeral fans. Men wore black suits and ties. A black wreath was hung on the door of the bereaved family's home, and all the mirrors were covered in black crepe. Most importantly, folks respected the privacy of families who had suffered loss. Like almost every aspect of modern life, however, send-offs these days are often short and sweet. Friends and family come by to offer covered dishes and sympathy, and those who mourn are expected to bounce back and get on with life, whether they are ready or not. But Jesus understands a broken heart and draws close to those who are hurting. He said, "Blessed are those who mourn, for they will be comforted" (Matthew 5:4 NIV).

FAITH CHECK

Mourning lays a crushing burden of separation upon us, but God lifts our burdens and cradles our hearts.

Our destination
is a place, far
greater than we
know. For some the
journey's quicker,
for some, the
journey's slow.

MEMORIAL CARD, VINTAGE

THE SWEETEST
OF THE SWEET

Pleasant words are like a honeycomb,
sweetness to the soul and health to the bones.

PROVERBS 16:24 NKJV

The welcoming parlors of the South are its tidy porches and sweeping verandas, complete with fans, ferns, and white wicker furniture. And no one can deny that sipping the thirst-quenching goodness of sweet tea on a lazy summer day is pert' near heavenly. But sometimes in the devilish heat, the desire to gossip or "spill the tea" to a friend or two creeps in and many a godly woman shares what shouldn't be spoken. Often the gossip is disguised as a call to pray. "We really need to pray for so-and-so. I heard she did this or that." Scripture instructs us to keep our tongues from evil and our lips from telling lies (Psalm 34:13). The next time you find yourself tempted to spill the tea, smile and take a sip of your sweet tea instead.

FAITH CHECK

A wise Southern woman once said, "It's always best to stop and taste your words before you let them pass through your teeth."

A real Christian is one who can give his pet parrot to the town gossip.

BILLY GRAHAM

HEAVENLY ASPIRATIONS

I am the door. If anyone enters by Me, he will be saved.
JOHN 10:9 NKJV

During a visit to the observation deck of the Empire State Building, tourists were astonished to discover ants. Granted, these ants were probably part of an ambitious high-rise colony that decided to "move up" in the world, 102 stories up, to be exact. But those tenacious little insects had worked hard nonetheless to reach such heights. One has to admire their determination.

Many of us are just as determined to reach heaven through sheer force of will and purpose, successfully scaling mountains of adversity and flying high on our own accomplishments. But like the ant, no matter how high we climb, we cannot reach heaven on our own strength. The only way to heaven is through Jesus, the Way through which each believer must pass into eternal glory.

FAITH CHECK

Are you tired of reaching for the stars? Then use your hands to knock instead. "So, I say to you, ask, and it will be given to you; seek, and you will find; knock, and it will be opened to you." (Luke 11:9 NKJV).

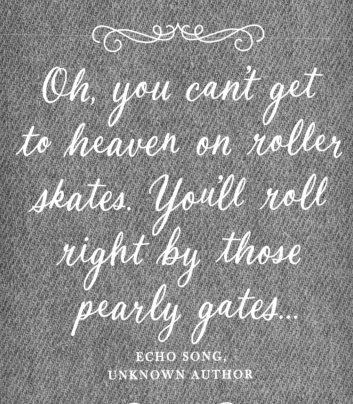

Oh, you can't get to heaven on roller skates. You'll roll right by those pearly gates...

ECHO SONG,
UNKNOWN AUTHOR

SMALL TOWN GLORY BOUND

And Nathanael said to him, 'Can anything good come out of Nazareth?' Philip said to him, 'Come and see.'

JOHN 1:46 NKJV

Soon after uttering that famous question, Nathanael became a disciple of Jesus Christ. But if he had based the decision to follow the Messiah purely on his bias toward Jesus's humble hometown, he might have spent a lot more time sitting under fig trees waiting for something to happen in his life. Most of us are impressed with titles, credentials, and backgrounds. We tend to look up to people who have incredible resumes and *vitae*, seemingly perfect people who are followed by a train of education, experience, and widely publicized good deeds. But how many times have we put someone on a pedestal only to be disappointed?

FAITH CHECK

People are easily impressed by titles, but God is not. Whether you are rich as a king or poor as a church mouse, whether you sit on a throne or a milk stool—it's not where you come from that matters, it's where you're going to spend eternity that counts. Where are *you* going?

The nice part about living in a small town is that when you don't know what you're doing, someone else does.

LIFE'S LITTLE HIGHLIGHTS

*Do not merely look out for your own personal
interests, but also for the interests of others.*

PHILIPPIANS 2:4 NASB

A fond memory many of us have about going to the doctor's office as children is the time we spent in the waiting room, for it was there that we had the opportunity to peruse the "Find the Hidden Pictures" page in *Highlights* magazine, delighting in each discovery of obscure items like tiny pencils, paintbrushes, toothpicks, and thumbtacks. How is it that we lose some of that skill as we grow into adulthood? Why do we sometimes miss signs of danger and clues that those around us are suffering? Because when we neglect to focus on anything but ourselves, we fail to notice the little details. And as they say, the devil is often in them.

FAITH CHECK

Remember the words of Sir Isaac Newton, who said of his own scientific discoveries, "If I have been able to see further, it was only because I stood on the shoulders of giants." For believers, to see beyond what is natural, we must stand upon the big shoulders of God and see things from His point of view.

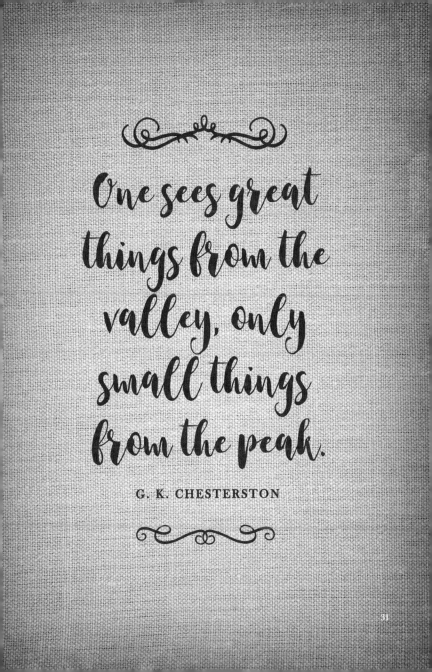

One sees great things from the valley, only small things from the peak.

G. K. CHESTERSTON

CHRIST OR CANAPE?

Now while they were on their way, Jesus entered
a village [called Bethany], and a woman named
Martha welcomed Him into her home.

LUKE 10:38 AMP

The two sisters of Lazarus, Mary and Martha, are often used as Sunday school examples. Jesus and His disciples had come to their house to visit. Martha's mind immediately went into hospitality mode, proving that she had a lot in common with a good Southern hostess. She got right to work making sure everybody was comfortable and had enough to eat. But Mary didn't lift a finger to help. Instead of helping, she plopped herself down at Jesus's feet. Frustrated and feeling sassy, Martha put her hands on her hips and asked Jesus, "Lord, do You not care that my sister has left me to do all the serving alone?" (Luke 10:40 NASB). Jesus acknowledged her worry and anxiety, and then to Martha's surprise, He defended Mary. "But only one thing is necessary, for Mary has chosen the good part, which shall not be taken away from her" (Luke 10:42 NASB). Jesus knew His time on earth was limited and that Mary had made the right choice to sit at His feet and hear what He had to say.

FAITH CHECK

Sometimes we can get so wrapped up in serving at church, we forget why we're there. Mary wasn't lazy like her sister thought. She knew when it was time to take her apron off and be still before God.

Worrying is like sitting in a rocking chair. It gives you something to do, but it doesn't get you anywhere.

ERMA BOMBECK

THIS LITTLE LIGHT

The city does not need the sun or the moon to shine on it, for
the glory of God gives it light, and the Lamb is its lamp.
REVELATION 21:23 NIV

In a popular magazine, a reader posed the question, How is it that we can look up at the sky on a cloudless night and see thousands upon thousands of stars, yet in pictures of Earth taken from space, our planet always seems to be shrouded in darkness? The answer is simple. The earth, when lit by the sun, is thousands of times brighter than the stars around it.

In the light of God's presence, we diminish as well. For believers, as bright as our little lights shine in the darkness of this planet, they will barely register a flicker in the presence of the glory of Jesus, the Light of this world.

FAITH CHECK

When the temptation arises to take pride in our accomplishments or achievements, we must remember and recognize that it is His light shining through us and directing our path that makes us shine, not anything in ourselves. As the brightness of the earth is a reflection of the sun, so our light is a reflection of the Son of God.

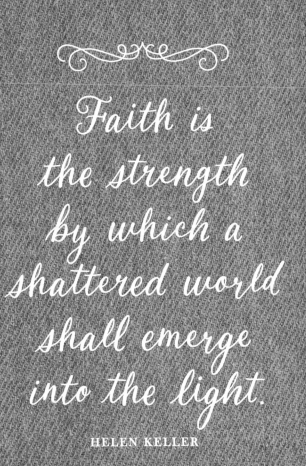

*Faith is
the strength
by which a
shattered world
shall emerge
into the light.*

HELEN KELLER

TRAINING GROUND

And his master saw that the LORD was with him and
that the LORD made all he did to prosper in his hand.

GENESIS 39:3 NKJV

Have you ever found yourself in a position completely opposite of where you hoped to be? Well, you're not alone. Joseph, a favored child, was sold into slavery by his jealous brothers and faced the prospect of a dismal life. Still, he made the most of his situation and excelled in his lowly state. Then things got even worse. Joseph was accused of a crime he didn't commit and was thrown into prison. Most people would be downright depressed at this point, mad at the world and mad at God. But he again found favor, this time with the prison warden, who entrusted him with important responsibilities. Afterwards, through another series of miraculous circumstances, God raised Joseph up to become Pharaoh's "right-hand man," and God ultimately used this former slave and prisoner to preserve the people of Israel during a great famine.

FAITH CHECK

You might find yourself in a difficult training ground as well, but be assured that the same God who prepared Joseph for great things is preparing you. A person who excels in his or her work will stand before kings (Proverbs 22:29).

Other people may have more talent, education, or experience, but God's favor can cause you to go places you could not go on your own.

DONNA PARTOW

MORE THAN ENOUGH

Seek the LORD [inquire for Him, inquire of Him, and require Him as the foremost necessity of your life].

ZEPHANIAH 2:3 AMP

If God were water, we would thirst for Him each day. If He were food, we would hunger for Him. If He were air, we would breathe Him into our lungs twelve to twenty times a minute. Yet God, our Creator, is all these things and more. If we need these basic necessities for our daily physical existence, why then do we so easily allow our spirits to starve by not opening our Bibles? When Jesus fasted and prayed in the desert for forty days, the devil tempted Him by urging Jesus to turn stones into bread. And even though Jesus was famished, He answered, "Man shall not live on bread alone" (Luke 4:4 NIV). There is more to this life than basic survival. Our bodies hunger for one thing and our spirits for another. Thankfully, God provides a daily portion for us through Scripture, which is manna for the soul.

FAITH CHECK

We all have problems in this life, worries, concerns, sad situations, and important decisions to make. Most importantly, we all have questions we need the answers to. To find "The Answer," open your Bible and read. Feed your spirit with good soul food!

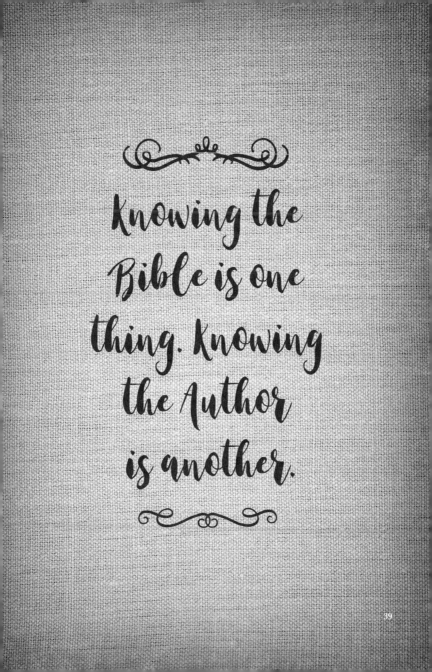

Knowing the
Bible is one
thing. Knowing
the Author
is another.

LONELY LITTLE PETUNIA
IN AN ONION PATCH

Love bears all things, believes all things,
hopes all things, endures all things.
I CORINTHIANS 13:7 ESV

Mothers are known to offer stern admonitions to daughters of dating and courtship age. "Don't drink. Don't chew. And don't go with boys who do." And wise words they are. But young men are clever with their words as well. Most young ladies would not be able to resist dating a charmer who drops a packet of sugar on the floor, picks it up, and says, "You dropped your nametag." A girl can look around all she wants for the right guy, a man of good character who is considerate, reliable, consistent, and committed, and still not find Mr. Right. It's easy to become discouraged or even depressed, giving in to the notion that there are no more good guys left in the world. But even if you feel like the last pea on the plate, rest assured, there are still some good guys around.

FAITH CHECK

In the Old Testament, young women trusted their parents to choose a proper spouse for them. But parents and children often have different criteria in mind. The best course is simple: pray and trust God to supply all your needs according to His riches in glory (Philippians 4:19) and go about your life until the right one comes along in God's time.

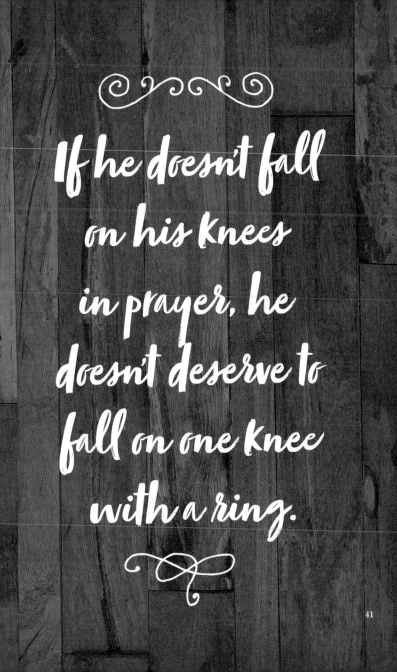

If he doesn't fall on his knees in prayer, he doesn't deserve to fall on one knee with a ring.

SPLISH SPLASH

Jesus said to him, "He who has bathed needs only to wash his feet, but is completely clean; and you are clean, but not all of you."
JOHN 13:10 NASB

Most kids don't like baths. But that crust of dirt behind their ears and remnants of moon pie swiped across an arm are begging for one. On their way to the rub-a-dub tub, mothers tell their kids like it is: "Wash up as far as possible. Wash down as far as possible. And then wash possible."

Now, even after a shower or bath, the moment one's feet hit the floor, they come into contact with the dust and dirt of the world. Believers are cleansed once and for all by the blood of Christ, but our minds need to be cleansed daily and renewed by diving into God's Word (Romans 12:2).

FAITH CHECK

Your mind, character, and attitude are revitalized, nourished, cleansed, purified, and sanitized by studying God's Word daily. Sort of a spiritual bath without the rubber ducky.

Bathroom Rules:
If it's up, put it down. If it's on, turn it off. If it's dirty, clean it. If you're taking a long time, hurry up.

THE DOLDRUMS

"For I know the plans I have for you," says the LORD. "They are plans for good and not for disaster, to give you a future and a hope."
JEREMIAH 29:11 NLT

Parts of the Atlantic and Pacific Oceans are affected by the convergence of two belts of trade winds, a low-pressure zone centered slightly north of the equator where the prevailing winds cancel each other out. Sail-powered boats and ships can get stuck in a place of utter stillness for days or weeks at a time. And time seems to move as slow as molasses in July. Some sailors call this area "the desert of the ocean," because the doldrums are also one of the hottest places on earth.

But you don't have to be stuck in the desert of the ocean to experience the doldrums. What can you do when you feel like you've lost your passion for the Lord and are hopelessly anchored in a dead calm?

FAITH CHECK

Smooth seas do not make skillful sailors. Yet there are times when we find ourselves in a motionless state, exasperated and crying out to God. To get moving again, we need the fresh wind of the Holy Spirit. We need to lift our eyes to heaven, and God will lift our sails and navigate us out of the doldrums of our spiritual lives.

The Bible is God's chart for you to steer by, to keep you from the bottom of the sea, and to show you where the harbor is, and how to reach it without running on rocks or bars.

HENRY WARD BEECHER

DON'T PITCH A HISSY FIT!

He who is slow to anger is better than the mighty,
and he who rules his spirit, than he who captures a city.
PROVERBS 16:32 NASB

We all fly off the handle sometimes, but there are some people who take their "upset" to a whole new level. In the South, that condition is known as a "hissy fit." And if you tell folks that you're "fixing to pitch one," warning has been served. The word *hissy* is likely derived from *hysterics*, a sudden burst of uncontrolled anger, which is known to result in an angry adult "cranky pants" tantrum. Now, witnessing a two-year-old having a tantrum in a big box store is hard enough to suffer through, but watching an adult pitch a hissy fit can be downright embarrassing. Children throw tantrums because they haven't yet learned how to deal with frustration, and the same is true for adults. Some of us never learned how to properly communicate our feelings or solve problems with others in a positive way. The good news is, these skills can be learned at any age.

FAITH CHECK

Those who do not practice self-control will be subject to whatever controls them. Uncontrolled anger can lead to some very bad decisions and unhappy consequences. Self-control is a fruit of the Spirit, "the fruit of righteousness that comes through Jesus Christ—to the glory and praise of God" (Philippians 1:11 NIV).

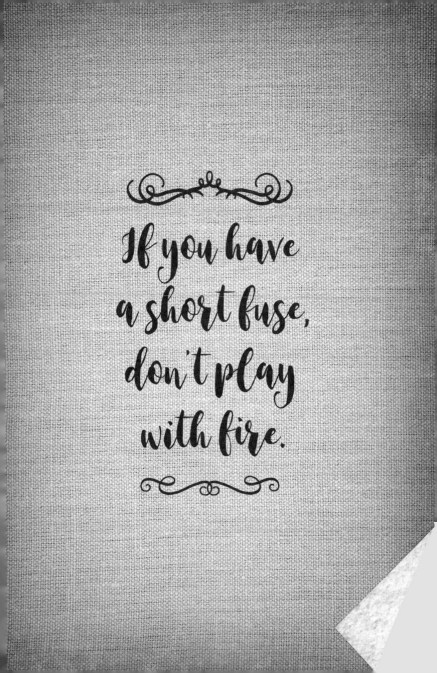

If you have
a short fuse,
don't play
with fire.

THE HAIR-AFTER

*The grass withers, the flower fades,
but the Word of our God stands forever.*

ISAIAH 40:8 NKJV

Beauty parlors are linoleum-floored social settings for Southern ladies, who favor high hair, hellacious amounts of hairspray, and beauticians they can count on as lifelong friends. Some beauticians style clients' "dos" from cradle to grave, making sure they look as good in the here-and-now as on their church send-off to the hereafter. But no matter how hard we try to avoid it, the day will come when gray hair will show up, cross its arms, and refuse to leave. And there won't be enough hair dye or nearly enough time to keep covering it. When the time comes to give up on the hair dye and highlights, get your style on. Then, lift your chin up, take a sip of your RC cola or that awful shoe leather coffee they serve in beauty parlors, and make up your mind that gray hair don't care! If you are blessed to live long enough, growing old is a part of life and age is a badge of honor, not a condition to remedy or be ashamed of. In fact, the Bible says gray hair is a crown of glory, gained by living a godly life (Proverbs 16:31).

FAITH CHECK

You can tease your hair as high as you want, but high hairdos won't bring you closer to God or heaven. Give God the glory for your "crown of glory," and rejoice in the beauty of your frosty season in life.

Gray hair is hereditary. We get it from our children.

SMOTE NOTE

And the angel gently smote Peter on the side and awakened him.
ACTS 12:7 AMP

U sually the word *smite*, or its past tense, *smote*, suggests an unpleasant experience to the one who is the object of the smote, because that person has been delivered a hard slap or a blow. But not always. Peter found himself thrown in prison by King Herod, guarded day and night and chained between two guards where he slept. But the church lifted up fervent prayers on Peter's behalf. God heard their prayers and sent an angel who "smote" Peter on the side with a gentle nudge to waken him. King Herod experienced quite a different sort of smote at a later time. Arrayed in the royal robes of the false Jewish king he fancied himself to be, and seated on an ornate throne, he delivered an eloquent oration to a crowd of adoring admirers, who shouted, "It is the voice of a god, and not of a man!" (verse 22 AMP). The saying must have pleased Herod, because he didn't stop the crowd from glorifying him instead of God. So, an angel of the Lord smote Herod and cut him down because he did not give God the glory that belongs to Him alone.

FAITH CHECK

Which kind of smote would you rather be the recipient of? A gentle nudge to awaken or a hard blow resulting in your demise? Consider this: we are all given a similar choice—to receive a gentle nudge to awaken us to God's truth of salvation or to depart suddenly in our sins, "where their worm does not die and the fire is not quenched" (Mark 9:48 ESV).

He who created us without our help will not save us without our consent.

ST. AUGUSTINE

LET'S HEAR IT FOR KUDZU!

Then the LORD arranged for a leafy plant to grow there, and soon it spread its broad leaves over Jonah's head, shading him from the sun. This eased his discomfort, and Jonah was very grateful for the plant.

JONAH 4:6 NLT

Kudzu is a climbing, coiling, perennial vine with an accelerated capacity for growth that is virtually unstoppable. Late in the nineteenth century, America's most infamous weed was introduced from Asia to the highways and byways of this country as a garden plant and a boon to agriculture. The invasive plant grows a mile a minute, eating up millions of acres of native plants and creating other-worldly landscapes of tangled, eerie-looking shapes. But hold on a minute—kudzu may not be all that bad. During times of drought, bees forage on kudzu nectar from the plant's grape-scented blossoms and produce a unique red or purple-hued honey that tastes like grape jelly or bubblegum. The plant can also be utilized as a food ingredient and for animal feed, basketry, clothing, medicine, toiletries, compost, and the production of ethanol.

FAITH CHECK

The plant that God prepared for Jonah to ease his discomfort in the heat of the fierce sun grew up overnight. God created that much-appreciated plant, and He created kudzu as well. Sometimes what we see as bad may actually be a benefit and boon to humanity.

Kudzu.
The vine
that ate
the South.

A WORK OF ART

But with the precious blood of Christ, as of a
Lamb without blemish and without spot.

I PETER 1:19 KJV

The true value of an object seems to lie more in the story or the individual behind it than in the materials used to produce it. Take art, for instance. In World War II, a Dutch art dealer sold Hitler's right-hand man, Hermann Goering, a famous painting by Vermeer for the equivalent of ten million dollars today. When World War II ended, Goering was captured and tried at Nuremberg, and it came out that the rare and precious painting that Goering had delighted in was a forgery, painted by the art dealer himself. Although everyone agreed that the painting itself was a masterful work, the forgery virtually undetectable except to a trained eye, it was of little monetary worth.

God knows the story behind each and every one of our lives and is well acquainted with every sordid detail about us, yet He holds us as precious treasures in His sight. God the Father paid a king's ransom to redeem us from our fallen state with His most precious possession, His only Son.

FAITH CHECK

The blood of Christ is the most precious gift we could ever hope to receive, and was offered to each of us absolutely free of charge. The story about this free gift can be found in the Gospels of Matthew, Mark, Luke, and John.

I would not give up one moment of heaven for all the joy and riches of the world.

MARTIN LUTHER

BEE CAUSE

I know that you can do all things, and that
no purpose of yours can be thwarted.

JOB 42:2 ESV

One of the most famous beekeepers of all time was Lord Baden Powell, founder of the Boy Scouts in England. Once, when preparing honey for a showing, the honey was allowed to overheat by mistake. But instead of tossing the "ruined" honey out, he decided to show the honey anyway, and as a result, dark honey became a fashionable new taste in England. Some of the greatest discoveries in this world came about as accidental inventions. A chemist discovered Teflon after an experiment went wrong. Super glue was a substance stumbled upon by accident by a scientist hoping to create a new precision gun sight. Play-Doh was designed to be a cleaning product for dirty wallpaper, until schoolchildren discovered it was perfect for craft projects.

FAITH CHECK

Many unexpected discoveries come from dismal failures. Though it is true that not all failures turn out well, each failure we experience in life teaches us what *not* to do next. Experience is what you get when you expect a different outcome.

Every man makes mistakes; they say a man who never makes mistakes never made anything else.

G. K. CHESTERSTON

Absalom, Absalom

When he cut the hair of his head . . . he weighed the hair of his head at 200 shekels by the king's weight.

II SAMUEL 14:26 NASB

It was said of David's handsome son Absalom that he had a truly luxurious head of hair. In those days, men grew their hair long, perfumed it with fragrant oils, and even powdered it with gold dust. Absalom had his hair cut once a year when he could no longer bear the weight of it—a whopping six pounds by most accounts! They say Esau was a hairy man, but put the two of them toe-to-toe, and Absalom would win the hair weight contest hands down. Absalom's father, David, was a man after God's own heart, but Absalom was arrogant, proud, and self-willed, and sought to seduce the hearts of Israel by false pretense in order to take his father's throne. In the battle that followed, Absalom found himself pursued by David's soldiers, and he escaped into the forest on a mule. However, as the mule passed under the thick boughs of a giant terebinth tree, Absalom's hair got caught on the boughs and "he was left hanging between heaven and earth" (II Samuel 18:9 NASB). There, the soldiers struck him down and he died.

FAITH CHECK

This is the fate of all those who forsake God. They are left helpless, caught between a heaven they will never know and an earth they will soon depart.

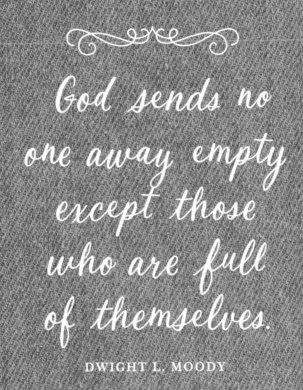

God sends no one away empty except those who are full of themselves.

DWIGHT L. MOODY

GIMME SOME SUGAR!

Be devoted to one another in love.
Honor one another above yourselves.

ROMANS 12:10 NIV

When a mama or a grandmamma or an auntie tells you, "Gimme some sugar," you can be certain she's not asking for a spoonful of sweet stuff for her coffee. She's asking for a big sloppy affectionate kiss. In the Bible, kisses on the cheek were a customary manner of salutation or mark of respect among relatives. In the early church, a kiss offered as a salutation was symbolic of wider Christian fellowship and brotherly love. Affection is a sweet and simple way to show those around you that you care.

There are many ways to show your affection for others. In the South, some people express their love through food. It is not uncommon for new neighbors to find a sweet potato pie or a casserole or even a delicious peach cobbler with homemade hand-turned vanilla ice cream at their door. Other people will mow your lawn when you're sick, or help pay your bills when you're out of work.

FAITH CHECK

Human contact and interaction are as necessary to life as food and water. Affection is a way of showing others they are important to us. Whatever way you show your love, through touch or food or thoughtful deeds, you are showing a fellow human being that you care about them. And that kind of sugar is the sweetest of all.

The love of
our neighbor
is the only
door out of the
dungeon of self.

GEORGE MACDONALD

The Hurrier I Get

Careful planning puts you ahead in the long run;
hurry and scurry puts you further behind.
PROVERBS 21:5 THE MESSAGE

We're all in a hurry these days. Our employers sometimes breathe down our necks to rush an important project through too quickly, often with poor results—proving the adage that there's never enough time to do it right the first time but always enough time to do it over again. In this age of instant everything, it is hard not to interpret God's delays as denials. We want what we want when we want it! Yet the discipline of delay is another expression of God's love for us.

The apostle Paul was a get-up-and-go kind of guy. He shared the gospel in at least fifty cities, and would likely have continued sharing if he had not been imprisoned. The energetic apostle must have wondered what possible good he could do stuck behind bars, yet in those quiet hours he was able to sit down and write his letters to the church. In the stillness of a sedentary life, Paul completed what God wanted him to accomplish, though he would likely never have imagined his sentence to be God's will for his life.

FAITH CHECK

We all think we know what's right for us, but God our Father truly knows what is best. Patience will perfect and prepare us for the work ahead.

What did the snail say when it was riding on the tortoise's back? Whee!

KIND EYES

*Leah's eyes were weak, but Rachel was
beautiful in form and appearance.*

GENESIS 29:17 AMP

Jacob was madly in love with Rachel, so much so that he agreed to work for her father for seven years with the understanding that the two would be allowed to marry. However, Laban was not about to let his younger daughter marry before the older one, so he pulled the old wedding night switcheroo on Jacob, who woke up to Leah and her "weak eyes." Was she nearsighted or farsighted? Plain or homely? Whatever was going on with her eyes, there was one thing she was not—loved. And Leah wanted to be loved more than anything, but Jacob only had eyes for her beauty-queen sister, Rachel.

FAITH CHECK

Favored by God, Leah was blessed with six sons and one daughter. The names of each of her sons reflect the emotional sorrow and frustration of her life until she gave birth to her fourth son, Judah, whose name means "This time, I praise Adonai." The pain of her plight ended when she decided to praise God in spite of her situation. And God's favor continued in her life, for the Messiah came through the lineage of Judah.

If you're trapped in a loveless marriage, you'd better learn how to make pie.

BLESS YOUR HEART!

Pleasant words are as a honeycomb,
sweet to the soul, and health to the bones.

PROVERBS 16:24 KJV

The phrase "Bless your heart" can be a wolf-in-sheep's-clothing kind of saying. "Bless your heart" can be a sincere expression of sympathy or a gracious-sounding grenade. When Southerners want to say something nasty about someone, they pour a little "word syrup" over the insult to make what they say sound downright polite. For instance, "Bless his little pea-picking heart. If brains were dynamite, he couldn't blow his nose," or "Bless her heart. She's so stubborn, she'd argue with a stop sign," or "Bless her heart. Granny cooked enough supper to feed Pharaoh's army." You can "say it nice," or "say it as vice," but "bless your heart" is an expression that is here to stay.

FAITH CHECK

Bad-mouthing is still bad-mouthing, no matter how sweetly one says it. The tongue has no bones but it has the power to break someone's heart. Our words should be as sweet as our tea. As the old saying goes, "If you can't say something nice about someone, say nothing at all."

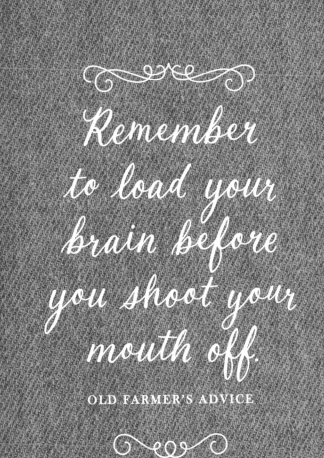

Remember
to load your
brain before
you shoot your
mouth off.

OLD FARMER'S ADVICE

THE UNWELCOMING COMMITTEE

I am the good shepherd. I know my own and my own know me.
JOHN 10:14 ESV

Have you ever walked into a room and felt about as welcome as a hair on a biscuit? When you're the new kid on the block, sometimes people look at you like an invading virus instead of a potential new friend. Cliques are everywhere, in neighborhoods, at work, even in churches. But what can you do when you're the odd one out? If you want fellowship, the first thing you have to do is get to know the fellows on the ship. Dale Carnegie, who wrote the classic book *How to Win Friends and Influence People*, said that learning a person's name is key. "Remember that a person's name is, to that person, the sweetest and most important sound in any language," he wrote. Next, listening is important. In fact, listening is half of any successful conversation. In short, be friendly, if you want to have friends.

FAITH CHECK

In the South, most people are friendly folks who generally view strangers as friends they haven't met yet. Whether you are part of a clique or a nervous newcomer, step out of your comfort zone and extend a hand of friendship. You'll be glad you did.

If you wanted
to feel at
home, you
should have
stayed there.

THE DEEPER THINGS

For the LORD sees not as man sees: man looks on the outward appearance, but the LORD looks on the heart.

I SAMUEL 16:7 ESV

A compliment is a genuine expression of praise or admiration, a simple act of thoughtfulness that can brighten any day. Flattery, on the other hand, is insincere and often excessive praise. It's easy for most of us to spot a flatterer because there's always something in it for them, for example, an employee telling his boss how great his new haircut looks when he knows full well his hair looks like it's been chopped with a weed whacker.

In contrast to insincere compliments, the apostle Paul's compliments to his fellow workers in Christ were of a spiritual nature, and completely selfless. In his letter to the Roman church (Romans 16:1–15), Paul begins by introducing Phoebe as a dear Christian woman who "has also been a helper of many" (verse 2 NASB). He follows with a long list of compliments for others: "Give my greetings to Tryphaena and Tryphosa, the Lord's workers, and to dear Persis, who has worked so hard for the Lord. Greet Rufus, whom the Lord picked out to be his very own" (verses 12–13 NLT). Paul's compliments likely encouraged and bolstered the confidence of those in the ministry with him and helped them to be better in the work God had called each of them to do.

FAITH CHECK

Instead of complimenting people on the way they look on the outside, why not take a cue from the apostle Paul and compliment them on their inner beauty?

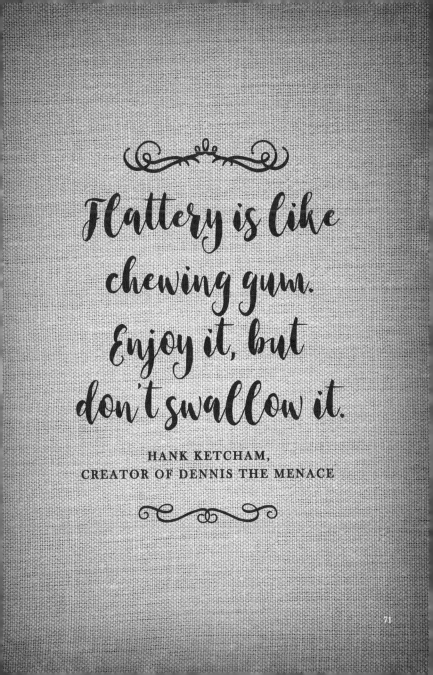

Flattery is like chewing gum. Enjoy it, but don't swallow it.

**HANK KETCHAM,
CREATOR OF DENNIS THE MENACE**

Good, Acceptable, and Perfect

And do not be conformed to this world, but be transformed
by the renewing of your mind, that you may prove what
is that good and acceptable and perfect will of God.

ROMANS 12:2 NKJV

People often ask what the difference is between God's good, acceptable, and perfect will. Instead of splitting hairs over that question, however, consider this: there are really only two choices in this world, to do good and to do evil. As believers, we know that God wants us to do good according to His Word, which He has given us. This is His will for our lives. Many people believe they are good, but *good* without *God* is irreconcilable. No one can pole vault from the earth to the moon, and no one is good enough or strong enough to get to heaven without God.

FAITH CHECK

God's perfect will for us is to follow Him, share the gospel message of salvation with others, and do His will on the earth. If we continue to follow Him and live according to His Word, the Bible, we will accomplish His perfect will in our lives.

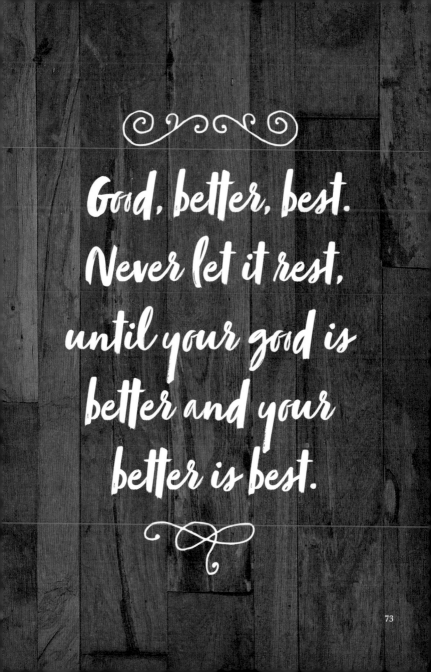

Good, better, best.
Never let it rest,
until your good is
better and your
better is best.

VINE OF MINE

But the fruit of the Spirit is love, joy, peace,
patience, kindness, goodness, faith, gentleness, self-
control. Against such things there is no law.
GALATIANS 5:22-23 HCSB

God described Israel many times in the Old Testament as a vine, and in time the vine became a cultural symbol for the nation, so much so that images of a vine were inscribed on their coins, art, and burial places. Vines in golden filigree adorned the entrance to the Lord's temple built by Herod. Jesus used the vine as an example of our relationship to Him. "I am the vine; you are the branches" (John 15:5 NIV). The secret of bearing fruit to God is abiding in Him, obeying Him, loving Him, and sharing that love with others. The Hebrew word for abide is to "stay, to make your home in, or dwell in." Abiding in Christ is a life of fruitfulness and abundance to God. Those who do not abide in Christ have no life in them and are like dead branches that will be pruned off and thrown into the fire (John 15:6).

FAITH CHECK

The fall of mankind began with forbidden fruit, but God bids us bear fruit to Him for the sake of mankind, for the furtherance of His eternal kingdom, and for His glory.

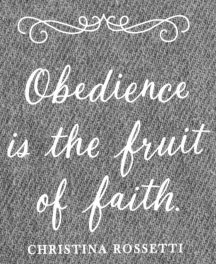

Obedience is the fruit of faith.

CHRISTINA ROSSETTI

THE WAY IN WHICH
WE SHOULD GO

Thy word is a lamp unto my feet, and a light unto my path.
PSALM 119:105 KJV

An estimated two to three million visitors hike portions of America's 2,181-mile Appalachian Trail each year. Hailed as the longest continuously marked footpath in the world, the Appalachian Trail is well-marked and well-maintained, but it is still easy to get lost on it. A stop for a bathroom break or to rest is all it takes for a tired soul to get turned around and lose their way.

With God as our Guide, we will always succeed in reaching our destination. The only way to completely fail is to ignore our Guide, the Holy Spirit, and the trail markers of God's Word. Choosing our own path is the way of destruction. Some people get lost and in trouble when they start out on the right path but decide to take a detour or two. God in His tender mercy never abandons those who are lost and want to find their way back. He is never far away from those with repentant hearts.

FAITH CHECK

Those who follow God stay close behind Him and set their feet in His very footprints. He illuminates the path before us and encourages us to stay on it.

If you board the wrong train, it is no use running along the corridor in the other direction.

DIETRICH BONHOEFFER

A SPOUSE IN THE HOUSE

Be completely humble and gentle; be patient,
bearing with one another in love.
EPHESIANS 4:2 NIV

Why do so many spouses look alike? There's the old saying that opposites attract, but do they really? The truth is, people are more attracted to someone who either looks like them or resembles their parents. We also look for mates with complementary personalities. Which means we're all sort of narcissistic in a way. Then there are married couples who didn't start out looking alike but over the years begin to look like they sprouted from the same family tree. Do we morph into our spouse from eating the same foods, or perhaps learn to mimic one another's facial expressions? Adam and Eve were completely compatible in every way. God not only created them for one another, but He actually made Eve from Adam's own rib. So, there's a high likelihood that the couple looked pretty similar and had a lot of spousal simpatico going on.

FAITH CHECK

Are couples simply similar because we choose someone who is like us, or do we begin to meld together with one another as a couple committed in Christ? As we mark the anniversaries that pass and the years that furrow our faces, perhaps the truth of successful marital relationships is not in the outward beauty that first attracted us but the inward beauty of surrendering ourselves to God and to each other.

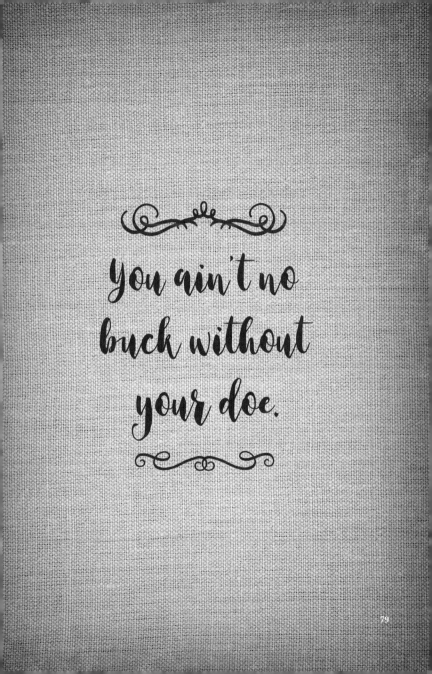

You ain't no
buck without
your doe.

THE FOUNTAIN OF YOUTH

*Your hair turns apple-blossom white...yes, you're well on your way
to eternal rest, while your friends make plans for your funeral*
ECCLESIASTES 12:5 THE MESSAGE

Spanish explorer and conquistador Juan Ponce de León supposedly came to the New World to look for the Fountain of Youth, a mythical spring that was supposed to restore the youth of anyone who drank of or bathed in its waters. But his discovery quest to what is now Florida in AD 1513 seems to be a myth itself. Though many an adventurous explorer has tried, no Fountain of Youth has ever been found. Remaining youthful in physical appearance is best left to the skills of plastic surgeons and the administration of Botox and fillers. If one lives long enough, however, no improvement will ever be enough to stave off the natural process of aging.

FAITH CHECK

Open an old church hymnal and one can sing a song written by William Cowper in 1771 about the glories of a very different sort of Fountain. "There is a Fountain filled with blood drawn from Immanuel's veins; and sinners, plunged beneath that flood, lose all their guilty stains...."

When you're young,
you think about dates.

When you're old,
you think about prunes.

SHOO FLY

And if I cast out demons by Beelzebub,
by whom do your sons cast them out?

MATTHEW 12:27 ESV

We've all played hide-and-seek with a haughty housefly before. And they seem to play along. Flies will buzz right past your head with a "what are you going to do about it?" attitude. They have a right to be so arrogant. A fly's eyes are more like a sensor array across their scalp, which is why it's so difficult to kill the icky little things. Not only can they see you coming with a trusty swat or rolled-up newspaper in your hand, they're fast as well. In fact, their wings beat up to two hundred times per second. Flies love to feast on garbage and many other gross things, contaminating surfaces they touch with thousands of germs, an amount that grows exponentially. Which is why, when you see a fly land on your cheeseburger at a cookout, you are likely to scowl in disgust. Dogs and cats are less discriminating. They catch these "sky raisins" in their mouths and eat them, which is ten kinds of nasty. Let's be honest, no one ever cried over a dead fly.

FAITH CHECK

In the Bible, the devil is referred to as "Lord of the flies" or "Baal-zebub." Is anyone surprised by that? After all, flies are attracted to death and decay and dung piles. The fourth plague God released on the Egyptians was swarms of flies (Exodus 7:20–31). Satan sends forth his demons to contaminate our lives with sin, sickness, and death, but the good news is, Jesus conquered sin, sickness, and death once and for all on the cross.

Time's fun
when you're
having flies.

KERMIT THE FROG

BICKERING WITH BEAKS

For though the LORD is high, He regards the
lowly, but the haughty He knows from afar.
PSALM 138:6 ESV

When it comes to chickens, birds of a feather do flock together. The status of each bird is established early in life, with the stronger chicks pecking at the weaker ones to mark their rank in the barnyard. Higher-ranking chickens get to eat and drink first and choose the best roosting spots. Chickens that look similar and are alike in breed, size, and health stick with one another. Birds that fall outside this category seem to be fair game for the rest of the flock to kill or even cannibalize. People, like chickens, try to establish a "pecking order" based on social status, finances, race, ancestry, or religion, and we often pick and peck at one another until we bloody and destroy others instead of accepting them and helping them out. But that kind of pecking order is the way of the world, not the supernatural, merciful order of God. "God resists the proud, but gives grace to the humble" (James 4:6 NKJV).

FAITH CHECK

Instead of destroying those who are weakest in the population, God calls us to do the opposite, to care for widows and orphans and the poor and, most of all, those who need Him. And whatever pecking order you find yourself in this world, you need Him too.

Wicked
chickens lay
deviled eggs.

THE CROSSROADS

*For what shall it profit a man, if he shall gain
the whole world, and lose his own soul?*

MARK 8:36 KJV

Described as melancholy music of African-American folk origin, blues music arose from slave songs and the harsh rural life of the Mississippi Delta. One of the most famous Delta blues musicians was Robert Johnson, and there is a legendary tale involving him—and the devil. In the 1920s, Johnson wanted to play the blues, but he was no good at it. So he disappeared for a time, and when he returned to the public eye, his music was different, described by many as extraordinary. When other musicians asked how he'd learned to play so well, Robert Johnson told them he'd gone out to the crossroads late at night, just before the midnight hour, and the devil showed up, offering to tune his guitar in exchange for Johnson's soul.

There are still those who sell their souls today for the things of this world, though what they gain in this life is temporary and what they lose is eternal.

FAITH CHECK

At a busy intersection in Clarksdale, Mississippi, is a marker composed of three huge guitars indicating the location where Robert Johnson purportedly sold his soul. But for believers, there is a more important sight to see. A hill known as Golgotha, where Jesus hung on a cross and gave His life to redeem our souls from death, hell, and the grave. Nothing this world can offer us is worth more than our salvation.

If we discover a
desire within us that
nothing in this world
can satisfy, also
we should begin to
wonder if perhaps
we were created for
another world.

C. S. LEWIS

POPULARITY

And He said to them, "Follow Me, and I
will make you fishers of men."
MATTHEW 4:19 NASB

Salmon swim against the current, migrating from the ocean to the upper reaches of rivers and on to the stream of their birth to lay eggs. This is known as the "salmon run" and it's popular with fishermen and bears alike. Any fisherman worth his salt knows that most fish swim against the current. Not only does this make it easier for fish to control their direction, it also takes less effort for them to snap up insects and worms. The food comes right *to* them.

Lots of public swimming pools now have what is known as a lazy river. You throw an inner tube into the water and plop yourself in the middle. You allow the current to take you around the relaxing course again and again until you're sunburned, and bored to tears. People without conviction or belief run the course of lazy thinking, going with the flow instead of confronting what is wrong and defending what is right.

FAITH CHECK

Swimming against the current of popular belief offers individuals the opportunity to sift through all the facts and opinions that come to them head-on, and to apply some critical thinking. And for believers, God's Word and prayer should always be a mainstay of that process.

Only dead fish go with the flow.

MALCOLM MUGGERIDGE

ALL THE RAGE

Do not let your adorning be external…but let your adorning be the hidden person of the heart with the imperishable beauty of a gentle and quiet spirit, which in God's sight is very precious.

I PETER 3:3-4 ESV

The beehive hairdo became all the rage after a woman named Margaret Vinci Heldt won the National Coiffure Championship in 1954. After that came mullets, mom jeans, shoulder pads, and stirrup pants. All of these fashion "don'ts" became popular because somebody introduced the look, which inexplicably became a hot trend. And of course, people bought 'em like hotcakes. Today, designer clothing and accessories—purses, shoes, belts, and even pet collars—sell at exorbitant prices. To add insult to injury, the designers print their names over everything. Think about that—we actually pay for the privilege of walking around advertising someone else's name on our bodies. They should be paying us!

Instead of looking like everyone else, why not develop a unique style of your own? A little style and creativity can go a long way. Too bad many of us missed this train of thought before the mom jeans and mullet thing . . .

FAITH CHECK

Instead of chasing after the latest "fa-fa, chic-chic" fashions, all of which will one day succumb to time and a whole lot of moths, we should adorn our hearts with the richness of a godly character. Besides, you already have a Designer and His name is written on your heart.

My room was
immaculate until
I decided to
match my shoes
to my outfit.

BAD THOUGHTS

Be angry, and do not sin; do not let the sun go down on your wrath.
EPHESIANS 4:26 NKJV

There are some folks in this world you just want to bless with a brick. Not literally, of course. But we sometimes think those kinds of thoughts when we're really mad. Bad thoughts are not sins, however. What we choose to do with those thoughts is what matters. Some people respond to these temptations by committing violence toward others. Sinners act on bad thoughts.

Jesus was in the synagogue when He came across a man with a crippled hand. He posed the question to those looking on, "Is it lawful on the Sabbath to do good or to do evil...?" (Mark 3:4 NKJV). No one said a word. Jesus looked around at them in anger at the hardness of their hearts, then He healed the man's hand. Jesus was angry, but He never sinned. So how could Jesus be angry? Because anger itself is not a sin. It's what we do with our anger that counts.

FAITH CHECK

The next time you're angry, give up your fighting stance and fall to your knees in complete surrender to God. Give up your anger, pain, and hurt to Him and forgive and pray for the person you're angry with. It is impossible to hate someone you continually pray for. Trust God who is completely righteous, for He promises, "I will contend with those who contend with you" (Isaiah 49:25 ESV).

Forgiveness releases the offense into the hands of God.

LYSA TERKEURST

THE FIRE
THAT BURNS WITHIN

Who among us shall dwell with the devouring fire?
. . .He who walks righteously and speaks uprightly.

ISAIAH 33:14-15 NKJV

While tending flocks near Mt. Horeb, Moses was drawn to what appeared to be a burning bush. Now, in the heat of the desert, it would not be uncommon to see a dry bramble bush spontaneously ignite, but this bush was different. The fire burned in the midst of the bush yet did not consume it. When Moses removed his sandals and drew near, God revealed Himself to Moses on that mountain. "I AM THAT I AM," He declared (Exodus 3:14 KJV).

Daniel's friends Shadrach, Meshach, and Adednego had a very different experience with fire. They were thrown into the midst of a blazing furnace for refusing to bow down and worship a pagan image. The blazing hot fire burned all around them but did not consume them or singe so much as a hair on their heads. Even King Nebuchadnezzar saw and recognized that the Son of God walked in the midst of the furnace with those three young men (Daniel 3).

FAITH CHECK

Our God is an all-consuming fire (Hebrews 12:29), refining us into pure, precious metal, burning away the dross of sin from our lives without destroying us. And the fire of His love ignites within our hearts—to testify, purify, and sanctify us to Him.

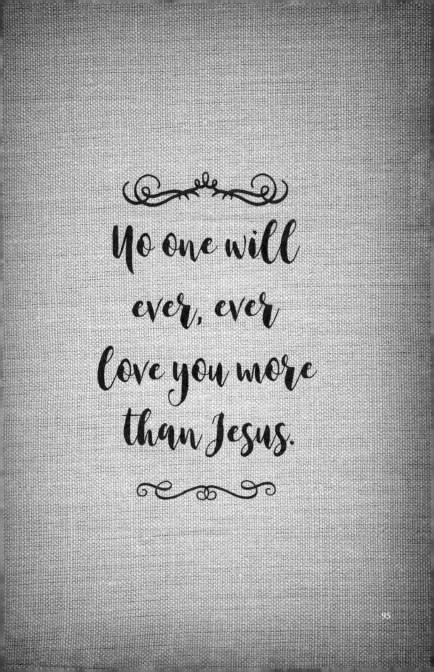

No one will ever, ever love you more than Jesus.

Beautiful Fluff

The righteous hate what is false, but the wicked make themselves a stench and bring shame on themselves.

PROVERBS 13:5 NIV

Anyone who has ever been around a cottonwood tree in early summer knows that white, ethereal fluff will soon begin wafting whimsically on the soft summer breeze. The female trees produce the fruit of the cottonwood in the form of a seed surrounded by a substance that looks like cotton, hence the name of the tree. Cottonwood trees are a beautiful sight to behold—unless you're an allergy sufferer.

In the age of electronic media, now available on every type of device imaginable, we are bombarded with all manner of news, like a rainfall of beautiful fluff, attempting to take root in our hearts. As believers, it is our responsibility to compare what we hear with the Word of God. The Bible is our standard to follow, to guide us into a right life with Him. But the fluff of the world is not worthy of a redeemed heart. The fluff of the world is only fit for the earth from which the tree sprang up.

FAITH CHECK

To avoid becoming the stuff of fluff, we must guard our hearts daily by studying the Word of God. If we know what is real, we will have no problem recognizing what isn't.

Listen to the murmur of the cottonwood trees.

DAVE STAMEY,
"DON'T FENCE ME IN"

FEEL THE HEAT

Choose you this day whom ye will serve.
JOSHUA 24:15 KJV

Southern climes are known for their triple-digit temperatures. Some days are downright hotter than a stolen tamale!

Did you know that Jesus actually prefers only two extremes in temperature—hot and cold? Lukewarm, not so much. Such was the city of Laodicea whose water supply came from a hot mineral springs about five miles from the city. By the time the water reached them via aqueducts, it was lukewarm, and it smelled like sulfur. Can you imagine what sweet tea made with sulfur water would taste like? Jesus said of Laodicea that their works were like their water supply, neither hot nor cold. With God, we need to let our yes be yes and our no, no! He gives us free will to either choose or forsake eternal life with Him. There are some folks who like "playing church" on Sundays and living like the devil the rest of the week. They never really commit their whole heart and their whole life to Him. Jesus finds this lack of commitment as disgusting as a mouthful of smelly, lukewarm sulfur water (Revelation 3:16).

FAITH CHECK

Sitting on the fence will never get you through the Pearly Gates. "Upon the wicked He will rain snares; fire and brimstone and a burning wind shall be the portion of their cup" (Psalm 11:6 NKJV).

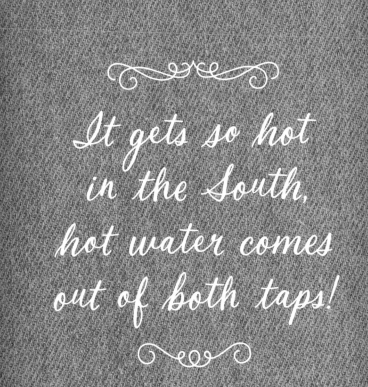

It gets so hot
in the South,
hot water comes
out of both taps!

BEFORE BEAUTY

*Stand up in the presence of the elderly, and show respect
for the aged. Fear your God. I am the LORD.*

LEVITICUS 19:32 NLT

There is a story from the late 1930s concerning famous debutante Clare Boothe Luce and Dorothy Parker, poet and satirist of the legendary Algonquin Round Table. The two women were trying to get out of a doorway at the same time when Clare drew back and said, "Age before beauty." Without missing a beat, Dorothy swept through the door, turned, and quipped, "Pearls before swine."

King Solomon wasn't very encouraging about old age in Ecclesiastes 12:3–4, when he said, "Your body will grow feeble, your teeth will decay, and your eyesight fail." In his later years, King Solomon wasn't what you'd call an encourager. Living in the twenty-first century presents a very different picture about growing old. We have medicine and physical therapy for arthritis, surgery for cataracts, and bifocals too. Dentures or implants solve those pesky teeth issues, and hello hearing aids! Thanks to better nutrition and healthy lifestyles, people can be in better shape and live longer lives.

FAITH CHECK

Our modern culture seems to favor the young, however, and shows little honor, patience, or respect to the older generation. Elderly people are made to feel as if they have no value or relevance, while the exact opposite is true. The longer you live, the more experience and wisdom you have to share. "The glory of the young is their strength; the gray hair of experience is the splendor of the old" (Proverbs 20:29 NLT).

I'm getting so old that all my friends in heaven will think I didn't make it.

NITPICKER

It is to one's honor to avoid strife, but every fool is quick to quarrel.
PROVERBS 20:3 NIV

Certain people are so persnickety, they could pick a fight in an empty house. Nothing ever satisfies or pleases them. Enough is never enough. They will find fault with you or a situation just to start up an argument. There's no peace with such a person. A conflict-free conversation is not possible, even about trivial matters. And the worst part is, they have little or no insight or self-awareness about what they do to those around them. It's their way or the highway. Nitpickers are not ruled by reason, persuasion, or self-control. With that said, absolutely anyone can be changed and transformed by the grace of God. The best way to deal with an argumentative fool is to stop wasting your time trying to defend yourself, and pray for them.

FAITH CHECK

Don't allow such a person to steal your peace or joy. Cease from arguing with them. That is what fuels their behavior. Instead, take all your frustrations to the Lord in prayer and praise.

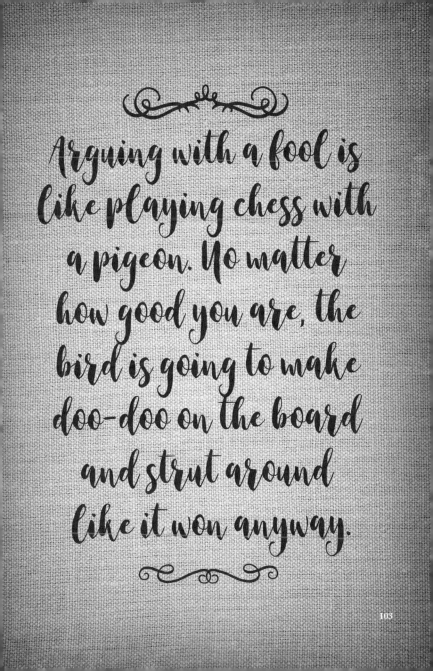

Arguing with a fool is like playing chess with a pigeon. No matter how good you are, the bird is going to make doo-doo on the board and strut around like it won anyway.

SIGN ME UP!

There is neither Jew nor Gentile, neither slave nor free, nor is there male and female, for you are all one in Christ Jesus.

GALATIANS 3:28 NIV

A message on a church sign tells it like it is: "Try Jesus. If you don't like Him, the devil will take you back." Shopping for a new church when you move to a new place is no fun at all. You put on your Sunday go-to-meeting clothes, shake a lot of hands, answer a mess of questions, and eat every variety of casserole known to mankind, all while smiling at strangers until your face hurts. On top of all that, every church wants you to fill out little cards with all your personal info. And you know what that means. Someone's going to start calling your phone or knocking on your door in a week or so.

Change can be difficult. It's easy to get frustrated and overwhelmed. Sometimes we long for our old church and pastor and all the familiar friends there, so much so that it becomes a chore, not a joy, to wake up on Sunday to kick the tires on another new church. But then one Sunday, everything changes. You're sitting in the pew minding your own business and somebody's singing a Sunday special up front, and the Holy Spirit does a tap dance on your heart. And you know, you somehow know that this church is your new home.

FAITH CHECK

Christians share the same Holy Spirit, so there is an instant familiarity with like-minded believers, but you know you're home when a certain church feels like family.

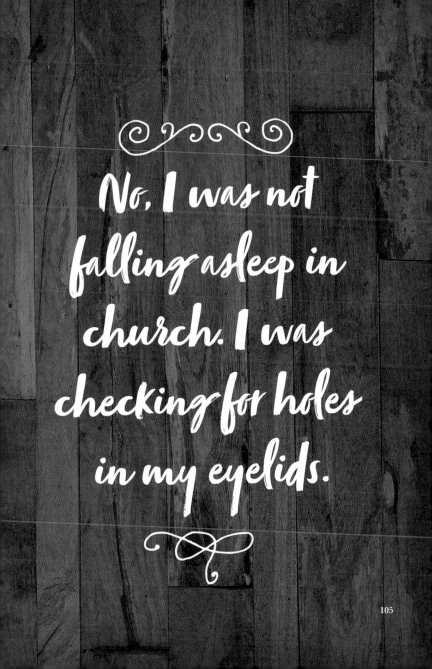

No, I was not falling asleep in church. I was checking for holes in my eyelids.

TALK IS TALK

*For the LORD gives wisdom; from His mouth
come knowledge and understanding*

PROVERBS 2:6 ESV

When someone says, "We done plowed that furrow clean down to the bedrock. Time to rest the mule," it means the matter has already been discussed way too much and it's time to move on. There are times in life when each of us must face major decisions, and people react to that burden in different ways. Some are good at snap decisions, and sometimes not so good. *Que sera* is their mentality. These folks are okay with whatever comes of their ill-thought-out and usually foolhardy plans, and they often get into trouble. Others like to mull things over, cogitate, ponder, deliberate, ruminate, dwell on, and talk about what to do over and over again until it makes your head hurt just listening to them. They refuse to act on a matter until they've planned and plotted out every scenario and result of the decision they fear to make. The word *fear* is important because the refusal to act is based in fear.

FAITH CHECK

What does the Bible say about decisions? James 1:5 (ESV) states, "If any of you lacks wisdom, let him ask God, who gives generously to all without reproach, and it will be given him." Asking God to give us wisdom in making decisions takes the pressure off us. When we invite God to be part of the decision-making process of our everyday lives, every decision, small or large, is made in partnership and reliance on God the Father.

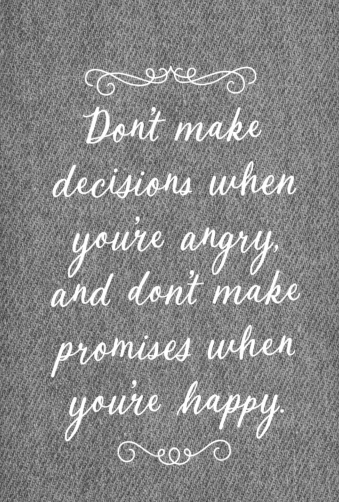

Don't make decisions when you're angry, and don't make promises when you're happy.

You've Got a Friend

John wore clothing made of camel's hair, with a leather belt around his waist, and he ate locusts and wild honey.

MARK 1:6 NIV

John the Baptist was a happy camper out in the wilderness of Judea. These days, people would pay a lot of money to wear camel hair anything, but John's camel's hair clothing was not what you'd call fancy, and likely was quite "aromatic." Food would've been hard to come by too. Eating honey fresh from the hive would certainly be pleasant, but can you imagine John the Baptist dipping locusts into the sweet, sticky stuff and crunching away?

Some people, like John the Baptist, prefer a little space away from civilization. They have a "Don't Fence Me In" kind of style, and that's okay. But if you live out in the deep country, way out in the boonies, you might feel overlooked, like you live on another planet. No one comes to see you. There aren't any exciting cities or towns near you. No airport hub either. And you alone are not enough reason to draw friends, even your own family, to visit you in the remote Timbuck-*three* area where you reside. You might as well make friends with a raccoon.

FAITH CHECK

There is, however, one faithful friend who will stick with you closer than a brother—like grits to a spoon: the Holy Spirit (Proverbs 18:24). No matter where you live or work, or where you go, He will always be with you and will never leave you or forsake you (Hebrews 13:5).

They lived so far
out in the country
that the sun set
between their
house and town.

Mama Bears

There are many virtuous and capable women
in the world, but you surpass them all!
PROVERBS 31:29 NLT

It is a well-known fact that mothers have eyes in the back of their heads and ears so sensitive they can not only hear a pin drop but also pick up on the slightest insurrection brewing among their children. And curious though it may seem, this auditory gift can be selective in its extent. Try asking mom for money. She will only hear the question when you've suffixed the sentence with, "And I'll do chores to earn that money." The slightest sound registered on a baby monitor will cause a new mother to bolt upright out of bed and dash to the baby's room. But veteran moms recognize the slightest variations between cries and know when to get up or slink back under the covers. If she senses you're in danger, a mama bear will roar to your rescue. A mama bear not only understands what her children say, she understands what they don't say. She will read your face like a police blotter, and though she loves you with an unconditional, fierce, protective passion, she will not hesitate to wallop your heart with the truth when you're wrong.

FAITH CHECK

Mothers never get enough sleep. They never eat a hot meal. And they love every minute of their life. Thank God today for blessing you with a mama bear.

You know you're a mom when you understand why the mama bear's porridge was cold.

RICH MAN, POOR MAN

*There was a certain rich man who was clothed in
purple and fine linen…and there was a certain
beggar named Lazarus, full of sores.*

LUKE 16:19-31 NKJV

Ever hear someone say of a wealthy person, "He's richer than Croesus"? Croesus was the king of Lydia in ancient Greece who was renowned for his massive wealth, so much so that his name became synonymous with riches and human vanity. He once asked Solon, the sage of Athens, to tell him who the happiest man in the world was, expecting him to drop Croesus's name, but Solon replied, "The fickleness of fortune means that the happiness of a man's life cannot be judged until after his death."

Jesus shared the parable with His disciples of Lazarus and the rich man. The rich man wore fancy clothes every day, but Lazarus was naked and covered with sores. The rich man ate gourmet meals every day, but Lazarus sat at the rich man's gate and begged for scraps from the rich man's table. Each man died and received his eternal reward, one in heaven and one in hell.

FAITH CHECK

Did you notice that Lazarus's name is noted with honor in God's Word but the rich man's name is not mentioned at all? Being rich or poor isn't a sin or judgment or desired situation in life. What we do with what we've been given, whether we bless others from a Croesusian treasury or offer a mere widow's mite, is what truly matters to God, for He judges the condition of the heart and remembers all that we do with it.

He's so rich he buys a new boot when he gets the other one wet.

EVEN MORE

I will become even more undignified than this, and
I will be humiliated in my own eyes. But by these
slave girls you spoke of, I will be held in honor.

II SAMUEL 6:22 NIV

When David and his retinue approached Jerusalem, celebrating the triumphant return of the Ark of the Covenant, David shed his royal robes and put on a Levitical-style ephod. With a joyful heart, he began dancing and leaping, offering a sacred dance before the Lord. When his wife, Michal, caught a glimpse of the dancing king from her window, however, she was embarrassed by her husband's lack of royal dignity and scorned him. When Michal confronted David about this, he answered, "It was before the LORD, who chose me above your father and above all his house, to appoint me as prince over Israel, the people of the LORD—and I will celebrate before the LORD" (II Samuel 6:21 ESV).

FAITH CHECK

For Michal's contempt of David's worship, God judged her and she did not bear children, but her barrenness was also symbolic of her lack of faith. Though she had once loved David, Michal didn't understand David's love for God and his unbreakable relationship with Him. She saw David's humble act of worship as foolishness. There may be those in your life who don't understand the passionate faith that guides your life, but those who love God and live to worship Him do not worry about looking foolish before others.

And I'll become even more undignified than this...

SINGER/SONGWRITER
DAVID CROWDER, "UNDIGNIFIED"

ONCE UPON A TIME

For the message of the cross is foolishness to those who are perishing, but to us who are being saved it is the power of God.

I CORINTHIANS 1:18 NIV

When company shows up and the temperature's less than scorching, a proper hostess will seat her guests comfortably on the shady side of the porch. She will soon return with a tray of chilled sweet tea and a plate of freshly baked cheese straws. When folks commence to talking, they might just start out with a Southern fairy tale, which usually begins like so: "Ya'll ain't gonna believe this . . ." In spite of the fairy-tale moniker, most of these stories start out as true-life adventures that somehow become embellished over time. Take fishing tales for example. The "caught fish" gets bigger every time the story is told.

True-life testimonies about what God has done in our lives are bigger than any twisted tale. Can you imagine the Israelites trying to explain to outsiders about the pillar of cloud by day and the pillar of fire by night? (Exodus 13:21). Or telling folks, "Ya'll ain't gonna believe this, but we don't need to go grocery shopping like you do. God our Father rains down this delicious stuff called manna that falls from the sky and we gather it up in our baskets every day and eat it."

FAITH CHECK

God is great and He does great things for us. Those who follow Christ know that answered prayers and miracles follow those who believe (Mark 16:17). And that's no fairy tale.

Life is not a
fairy tale.
If you lose
your shoe
at midnight,
you're drunk.

MUSICAL DISABILITIES

*Now these are the last words of David . . . the anointed
of the God of Jacob, the sweet psalmist of Israel.*

II SAMUEL 23:1 ESV

Praise and worship music go together and help bring us together into God's presence. In addition to all his other titles and achievements, talents and abilities, King David was a gifted musician, singer, and composer, so much so that he was known as "the sweet psalmist of Israel." He is credited with writing half of the songs in the Book of Psalms, which is a book in the Bible of sacred songs and prose. Before he became king, David was the official musician in King Saul's royal court. Whenever an evil spirit of jealousy tormented the king, David would strum his harp and sing soothing songs to calm him down. But sometimes when the king was "in his cups" and the evil came over him, David had to dodge more than a few spears launched his way. A tough gig, for sure.

William Congreve, a British author of the late seventeenth and early eighteenth centuries, wrote, "Music has charms to soothe a savage breast." One thing's for certain, music worked wonders at soothing King Saul when he had a spear in his hands.

FAITH CHECK

Many a doting mother has signed her child up for music or singing lessons, only to discover that their kid can't carry a tune in a bucket. We can't all be worship singers, but we can all worship together in church.

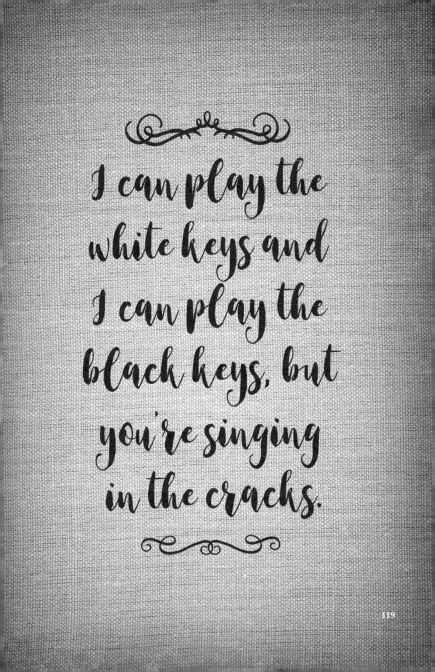

I can play the
white keys and
I can play the
black keys, but
you're singing
in the cracks.

BACK TO EGYPT

*The Israelites said to them, "If only we had died
by the LORD's hand in the land of Egypt, when we sat
by pots of meat and ate all the bread we wanted."*

EXODUS 16:3 HCSB

God bless the brave men and women who teach driving skills to young adults. They truly deserve medals for their valiant efforts, mostly because they save parents from having to sit in the passenger seat, fearfully pumping an imaginary brake with one foot. Many a driving teacher has admonished a new driver from constantly looking backward, "Don't keep looking back. You're not going that way."

Isn't that true of life as well? When we constantly look back, longing for something or somebody or the life we used to have, we are deluding ourselves. We can't live in the past. We can't live in the future either. The only time allotted to us in this life is the moment we are living in right now.

FAITH CHECK

The Israelites, though miraculously released from 430 years of captivity, actually preferred going back to life in captivity as slaves of Egypt because they were afraid that the God who parted the seas for them wouldn't provide food for their growling stomachs. They didn't appreciate what they had in the moment. Sure, freedom looked like a desert, but God was with them in that desert. And God is with you wherever you are, wherever you were, and where you are going.

Whether your glass
is half-empty
or half-full,
be thankful that
there's something in it.

Smellin' a Felon

Do not love the world nor the things in the world.
I JOHN 2:15 NASB

When someone steals something from you, there's a sensation of feeling violated, and you absolutely were. Your trust in humanity has been breached. Something that belonged to you was taken, and you might never see it again. Toddlers trust one another with a sweet innocence that is truly heartwarming to witness, until one day one little one decides to take another's toy. The situation goes south real fast. Trust is breached and those toddlers suddenly turn into angry, possessive monsters. Even if we're wise to the ways of the world, there is a part of us that wants to trust, and to be worthy of trust. We cannot allow ourselves to become angry or distrustful of everyone because we've been hurt by a few. Some people will make bad decisions, but the decisions in your life are all up to you.

FAITH CHECK

No matter how smart or stealthy a thief is, he will eventually slip up and be captured and punished. Even if you trust with one eye open, continue to trust. Don't allow the bad apples of the world to steal your peace and joy. Instead, place your confidence in Christ alone. Live in faith, not fear.

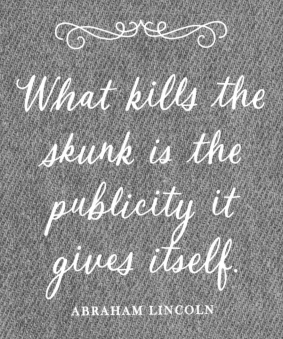

What kills the skunk is the publicity it gives itself.

ABRAHAM LINCOLN

DISCERNMENT'S
DOUBLE TROUBLE

So give your servant an understanding heart to judge
Your people to discern between good and evil. For
who is able to judge this great people of Yours?
I KINGS 3:9 NASB

Some people have a great sense of intuition. Their instincts for business, trends, or danger are spot on. In contrast, discernment is the ability to grasp and comprehend what is obscure, to choose between right and wrong. Godly discernment can only come from God. We are not born with spiritual discernment; we are *born again* into it. But if you pray for God to give you a discerning heart, know that your greatest weakness will stand right beside your greatest spiritual gift. Alongside the gift of discernment is the temptation to judge others based on what you know about them, yet God does not call us to judge but to pray and intercede—*and love.*

FAITH CHECK

King Solomon was gifted with Godly wisdom and was given authority to judge his people. For many years he judged rightly, but for some reason he could not discern between good and evil in his own life. Wisdom and discernment won't do us or anyone else any good if we cannot apply them to our own lives as well.

If you judge
people, you
have no
time to
love them.

How You See It

Yet God has made everything beautiful for its own time. He has planted eternity in the human heart, but even so, people cannot see the whole scope of God's work from beginning to end.

ECCLESIASTES 3:11 NLT

Some of the latter paintings by famous impressionist artist Claude Monet reflect the more vivid colors he was able to perceive after his cataract operation. He saw the world with one set of colors one day, and the next, he saw through a new color wheel that turned his life, and his art, around.

We live in this world with extraordinary diversity in people, animals, plants, colors, and so much more. Yet none of us are prepared for what we will see in heaven! We will marvel at vistas and landscapes we could never conceive of or imagine in our finite state. We will see new flowers and colors and live in the unfiltered light of God. Jesus has prepared a place for each believer and adorned it with His love.

FAITH CHECK

First Corinthians 2:9 (KJV) says, "But as it is written, eye hath not seen, nor ear heard, neither have entered into the heart of man, the things which God hath prepared for them that love Him." What we see now is a mere reflection in a dusty mirror, but one day we will see and understand all things clearly.

We look up at
the same stars
and see them
differently.

THAT DOG WON'T HUNT

*So it will be at the end of the age. The angels will go
out, separate the evil people from the righteous.*
MATTHEW 13:49 HCSB

Catahoula leopard dogs with their marbled-glass eyes and merle coats are native to Catahoula Parish, Louisiana. They are profound hunting dogs, and they owe their excellent skills and traits to careful breeding and culling. Puppies and grown animals who did not show promise as potential working dogs were eliminated. It is a difficult and seemingly barbaric practice for modern people to understand, but in those days, every animal the settlers provided for from their meager supplies had to provide for them as well.

FAITH CHECK

Jesus used parables to convey important truths to us. Whether He spoke of the wheat and the tares or separating the sheep from the goats, the message was clear. At the end of the age, God will separate the righteous from the unrighteous— culling away the unrighteous to everlasting punishment and the righteous to life eternal.

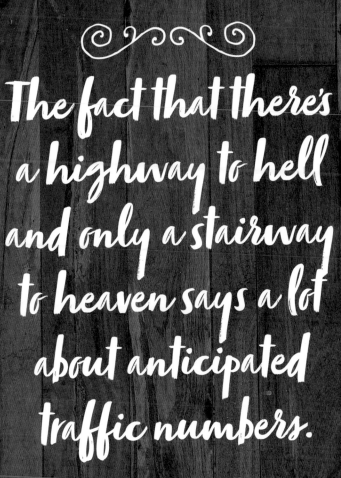

The fact that there's a highway to hell and only a stairway to heaven says a lot about anticipated traffic numbers.

HOWARD PITTMAN

THE LEAST YOU CAN DO

*And whoever gives to one of these little ones. . . even
a cup of cold water because he is My disciple, surely
I declare to you, he shall not lose his reward.*

MATTHEW 10:42 AMP

Anyone who has experienced Southern hospitality knows what it is to receive a warm, sweet welcome with a generous helping of good food! The Israelites said much in praise of hospitality and believed that to offer food, drink, and lodging to someone would bring a blessing upon their own home, as is the case with the house of Obed-Edom, where David lodged the ark for a time (II Samuel 6:11). For his hospitality, the Lord blessed Obed-Edom's household and everything he had, including his family, land, and livestock. He prospered in every way a person can prosper.

To help others in time of need can also bring the blessings of success, protection, and happiness to the one who blesses. Jesus said that to offer a disciple of Christ even a cup of cold water, which even the poorest among us can afford to give, would also be rewarded.

FAITH CHECK

The very least any of us can do to help others is to offer a cup of cold water to someone who thirsts, and the most we can do to help others is limitless, according to the abundance of the heart.

Every good
friend
was once a
stranger.

Toot Your Own Horn

*Let another praise you, and not your own
mouth; a stranger, and not your own lips.*

PROVERBS 27:2 ESV

Tooting one's own horn," better known as bragging, is not
so much an art as a vice. "Braggadocious" offenders are
everywhere—in Christmas letters, on social media, in politics,
in Hollywood, on bumper stickers, on playing fields, and
at weddings, funerals, and get-togethers, even in our own
families. Some people rave on and on about who they are—
their own accomplishments, how good they are at their jobs,
their honors and awards, their academic excellence starting
from kindergarten, or even how fantastic "they imagine" they
look physically. Other people brag about what they have—
their trophy wife, perfect children, designer clothing and
accessories, finances, home(s), automobiles, boats, or their
expensive trips and vacations. And some are super stealthy
about the *way* they brag. "I can't believe how small the cup
holders in the new Mercedes are."

The apostle Paul said we shouldn't brag about ourselves
but about Christ. "As for me, may I never boast about
anything except the cross of our Lord Jesus Christ. Because
of that cross, my interest in this world has been crucified, and
the world's interest in me has also died" (Galatians 6:14 NLT).

FAITH CHECK

A fool tells you what he will do, and a boaster will tell you
what he has done. But a wise man does it and says nothing.

When you're bragging, you're dragging.

JESUS KNOWS

And some of them began to spit on Him and to blindfold
Him and to beat Him with their fists, and to say
to Him, Prophesy [by telling us who hit you!].

MARK 14:65 AMP

When Jesus was taken before the Sanhedrin and asked if He was the Messiah, He told them, "I AM; and you will see the Son of God seated at the right hand of Power (the Almighty) and coming on the clouds of heaven" (Mark 14:62). Infuriated with self-righteous zeal, they condemned Jesus to death. To taunt Him, they blindfolded Him and demanded He tell them who punched Him repeatedly in the face. But Jesus knew exactly who hit Him. And He knew everything about every person who loved or hated Him. And He knew the number of every hair on the heads of the men who nailed Him to the cross. Yet He still chose to give His life for all of us, for sinners condemned to eternal death, that we might live.

FAITH CHECK

This is the definition of perfect love—that Jesus died *for* our sins that we might die *to* sin.

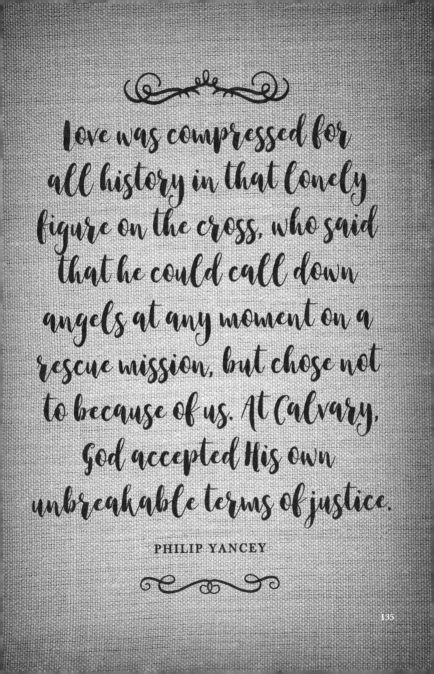

Love was compressed for all history in that lonely figure on the cross, who said that he could call down angels at any moment on a rescue mission, but chose not to because of us. At Calvary, God accepted His own unbreakable terms of justice.

PHILIP YANCEY

VENT UPWARDS

*Anyone who says he is a Christian but doesn't control his sharp
tongue is just fooling himself, and his religion isn't worth much*

JAMES 1:26 TLB

From time to time, we all feel the need to vent our emotions to a discreet and trusted friend, and there is nothing wrong with doing so. A good friend is a precious treasure who can lend an ear to listen and a shoulder to cry on. But how much better is it to take our problems to the throne, where God can truly help us. If venting, and ranting, and spewing emotion all over the place sounds kind of messy, it is. Especially if we pour out our frustration in front of other people or on social media. Remember, hurting people wind up hurting others. Proverbs 18:2 (ESV) says, "A fool takes no pleasure in understanding, but only in expressing his opinion."

FAITH CHECK

The truth is, we feel the need to vent because of a perceived injustice of some sort. However, if we believe the God we serve is a righteous God, then we should trust that His intentions regarding the situation will ultimately prevail.

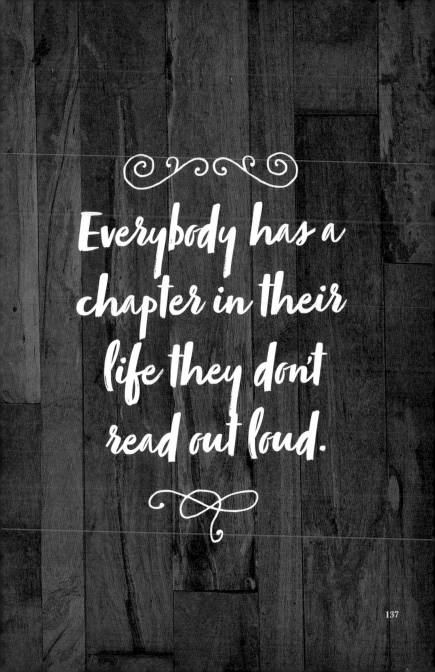

Everybody has a chapter in their life they don't read out loud.

THE TOWER OF SILOAM

For He makes His son rise on the evil and on the good, and sends rain on the just and on the unjust.

MATTHEW 5:45 NKJV

When disaster strikes, we often wonder why God allows it. Some people even direct their anger and accusations toward Him. But this is nothing new. The tower of Siloam was next to the pool of Siloam, and in between was a colonnade that connected the shared pool of Bethesda. Sick and disabled people congregated around these pools with the hope of receiving healing. One day the tower collapsed, taking eighteen of those souls. People had questions for Jesus about why these good people died. He replied, "Were they the worst sinners in Jerusalem? Not at all! And you, too, will perish unless you repent" (Luke 13:4–5 TLB).

FAITH CHECK

Jesus went straight to the heart of the matter—the state of the souls who died so tragically. Disasters do not discriminate and do not offer anyone the favor of warning. We need to be ready by knowing our Maker in the here and now before we meet Him face-to-face in the hereafter.

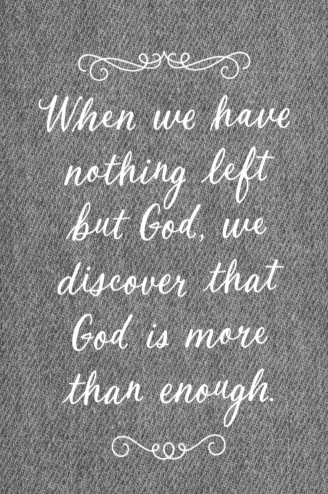

When we have
nothing left
but God, we
discover that
God is more
than enough.

How Much More?

If you then, though you are evil, know how to give good gifts to your children, how much more will your Father in heaven give the Holy Spirit to those who ask Him!

LUKE 11:13 NIV

Suppose a friend rang your doorbell in the middle of the night asking for a loaf of bread. Now, if a friend were in real trouble most of us would gladly, if not sleepily, give them whatever they needed. But wake you up for a lousy loaf of bread in the wee hours of the night? You would likely be aggravated with that friend for disturbing your sleep and waking your entire family, including your pets. You'd want to turn over and go back to dreamland. But you can't because that pesky friend just keeps on knocking on your door. So, you grudgingly come downstairs in your pink hippopotamus pajamas, grab the bread from your pantry, hand it over, and send that friend on their way.

FAITH CHECK

Jesus shared this parable as an example of persistence in our prayer life. A *fortiori* parable in the Bible is one that poses the question "How much more?" If we can be obstinate enough to ask others for help, we must also be obstinate enough to continue in our prayers and requests to God, who, so much more than a fickle friend, will give us what we need. Plus, God never sleeps, and He certainly doesn't wear pink hippopotamus pajamas.

*A friend
in need is
a friend
indeed.*

JOHN HEYWOOD

AND HE DID EVIL

*Ahab son of Omri did more evil in the eyes of
the LORD than any of those before him.*

I KINGS 16:30 NIV

You know an Old Testament ruler is bad when a Bible passage starts out with ". . . and he did evil in the sight of the Lord." Ahab was that kind of king and more, because he had the dubious distinction of "doing more evil in the sight of the Lord than any of those before him." It all started when Ahab married Jezebel, who was fanatical about her pagan gods and made it her business to establish a new state religion in Israel. At the same time, she began to stamp out the worship of Jehovah, murdering Israel's prophets and forcing others into hiding. Only the prophet Elijah stood up to her. God gave Elijah a great victory when he called down fire from heaven and destroyed the four hundred pagan prophets of Baal who came against God. Was everything perfect and peachy-keen after that? Hardly. Elijah had to run for his life. In time, though, Ahab and Jezebel met bitter ends as God executed justice for their sins.

FAITH CHECK

God will raise up either an Elijah or an Esther (Esther 4:14) for such a time as this. He will not tolerate sin or injustice among His people for long. "The LORD is your mighty defender, perfect and just in all His ways; your God is faithful and true; he does what is right and fair" (Deuteronomy 32:4 GNT).

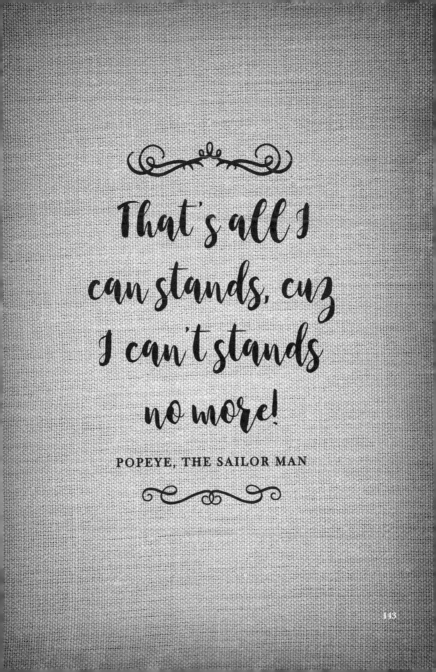

That's all I
can stands, cuz
I can't stands
no more!

POPEYE, THE SAILOR MAN

THE LAST SUPPER

While I was with them in the world, I kept them in Thy name;
those that Thou gavest me I have kept, and none of them is lost,
but the son of perdition; that the scripture might be fulfilled.

JOHN 17:12 KJV

Jesus knew full well that Judas was going to betray Him, yet He knelt down and humbly washed Judas's feet as He did with the other disciples. Imagine that. Jesus washed the feet of the man who sold His life for thirty pieces of silver. If you were Judas, what would be going on in your head at that moment? Think of it. The man you plan to betray, the Son of God, the Messiah, humbles Himself to the role of the lowliest servant and washes your feet. Would this act of love have given Judas pause? Or did this confirm in his mind that Jesus was not the sort of king Judas hoped he was?

FAITH CHECK

Although Judas took the bread and the wine of communion with Jesus and the other disciples, he was already involved in an unholy communion with the devil. Judas would never again sup with the Lord or experience the light of His tender love. Both men were about to die, one for the salvation of the world and the other to shame, dishonor, and eternal damnation. Jesus washed the earth from Judas's feet, but Judas would not allow the Savior of all mankind to wash his heart.

Don't fear the enemy that attacks you but the fake friend that embraces you.

THE NEED TO LEAD

Therefore, since we are surrounded by such a great cloud of witnesses, let us throw off everything that hinders and the sin that so easily entangles. And let us run with perseverance the race marked out for us.

HEBREWS 12:1 NIV

Which would you rather be, a leader or a follower? Most people would say they want to be a leader because leading seems much more important. And following sounds so namby-pamby. But when Jesus called His disciples, He said, "Come, follow me" (Matthew 4:19 NIV). Following Christ is the first step to success. The second is to join with other believers, the great cloud of witnesses, who will cheer you on and whom you also will cheer on. Next, let go of sin and worldly hindrances that are holding you back or dragging you down. Finally, don't quit before you reach the finish line!

FAITH CHECK

In this world, the way up the ladder to success is by any means necessary, often at the expense of others. But the way of the gospel is to work hard and succeed God's way, and to consider others before yourself. You can't climb the ladder of success wrong by wrong.

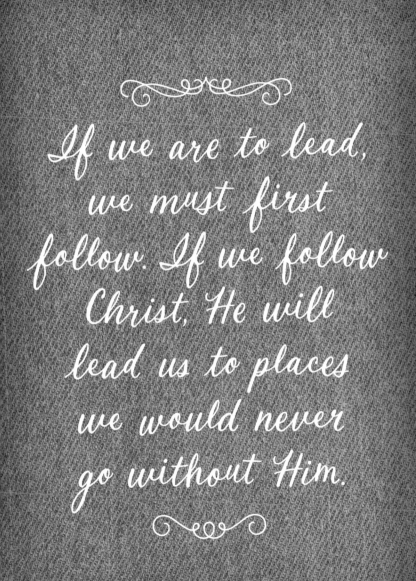

If we are to lead, we must first follow. If we follow Christ, He will lead us to places we would never go without Him.

147

TEARS IN A BOTTLE

*You have taken account of my wanderings; put my tears
in Your bottle. Are they not recorded in Your book?*

PSALM 56:8 AMP

A prisoner in Gath, David was at the lowest of lows in his life. The Philistines had captured him and he felt completely helpless. He called out to God in his sorrow and said that God put his tears in a bottle. Was there really such a bottle filled with David's tears? And does God save our tears in bottles as well? Regardless of whether or not God collected David's tears in a bottle, or collects ours as well, He certainly remembered David's sorrows as He remembers all our weeping. He remembers everything that we endure for His sake on this earth. And someday He will wipe away every tear from our eyes and there will be no more death, or mourning, or crying, or pain (Revelation 21:4).

FAITH CHECK

Some believe that in Victorian times, women in mourning carried around small ornamental blown glass bottles decorated with silver and pewter. Those mourning the loss of a loved one would collect their tears in these bottles called "tear catchers," or "tear bottles." As their tears evaporated with the help of special stoppers on the bottle, the mourning period would end. Someday, *our* period of mourning will end and we will forever be with our Father in heaven.

Tears are prayers from the heart when we cannot speak.

SNOW GLOBE FAITH

Don't be afraid, for I am with you.
Don't be discouraged, for I am your God.
ISAIAH 41:10 NLT

In the middle of a winter snow storm one year, a weather reporter warned listeners about "peep hole driving." With snow falling fast, ice could build up, blanketing car windows so heavily that drivers would soon find themselves desperately trying to see where they were going through a small porthole in the windshield.

How many of us live like that every day? We have a "tunnel vision" approach to life, preferring to press on in dangerous situations or circumstances and ignoring the gentle and sometimes stern warnings of the Holy Spirit. Of course, even on the best of days, our vision is limited. But our Father God is all-powerful, all-knowing, and everywhere at all times. Nothing escapes His sight, no detail or danger or plan of the enemy against us. Has your life and your faith been shaken recently? Do you feel like you're trapped in your own personal snow globe and can't see two inches in front of you? The good news is, there is an infallible way to settle that storm and set you free.

FAITH CHECK

Call out to God the next time you find yourself trying to press on in dangerous circumstances. He will either clear your path or clear your windshield.

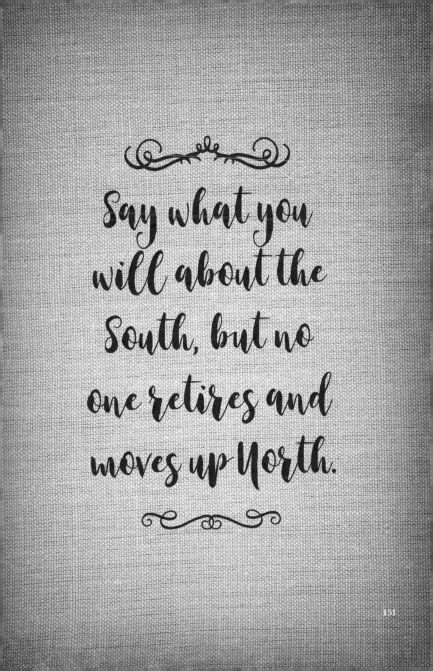

Say what you will about the South, but no one retires and moves up North.

GRANDMAS ARE MOMS
WITH LOTS OF FROSTING

How sweet are your words to my taste,
sweeter than honey to my mouth!
PSALM 119:103 ESV

I love you a bushel and a peck . . ." Grandmas love singing that song to their grandchildren. Whether you call her Grandmother, Grandma, Grannie, Grammy, Grams, Granna, Nana, Nonna, Noni, Bubbie, Abuelita, MawMaw, MeeMaw, Mimi, Gigi, or Momo—grandmas are special and they make their grandchildren feel special too. Grandmothers give the impression that they've been waiting to see their grandchildren all day, and they are completely enthralled with everything their little nuggets do. They hang on their little ones' every word and listen attentively to whatever they have to say. Grandmothers will read to children as long as they want. And when grandchildren visit, they know they are going to get three things—hugs, kisses, and home-baked cookies! Grandmothers always make sure children wear clean underwear and wash behind their ears too. And most importantly, they will listen to a grandchild's problems while they snap green beans together at the kitchen table.

FAITH CHECK

They say that a grandmother is a mother who has a second chance. Being a mom is stressful and busy, and oftentimes moms don't have extra time or patience with their children. As the years go by, however, most moms wish they'd done a few things differently with their children, and they are more than eager to pour out all their love and attention on their grandbabies.

It's such a grand thing to be a mother of a mother. That's why the world calls her grandmother.

GRITS AND GOD

By your endurance you will gain your lives.

LUKE 21:19 ESV

"Want some grits with those eggs?" The word *grits* doesn't sound all that appealing, but in Southern diners, the very mention of them gets a stomach to growling—in a good way. Regular grits are either white or yellow, with yellow grits being a bit sweeter and white grits offering up a subtle, velvety flavor. Southerners like their grits served swimming in butter, with syrup, or in the form of cheese grits, which are basically grits with butter, heavy cream, cheese, and a sprinkling of crisp crumbled bacon.

There's more than one way to prepare grits, and there's more than one meaning of the word *grit*. Take the expression "true grit," for instance. A person with true grit is someone who perseveres through challenges and sticks to their guns, regardless of failures or setbacks. They passionately follow after their goals with unwavering courage and purpose.

FAITH CHECK

A man or woman with true grit is a person of indomitable spirit. Who fits that profile in the Bible? Noah is one. He continued building the ark for over half a century while everyone mocked him. Abraham and Sarah believed God's promise that Sarah would conceive and bear a child at ninety years old. Moses went back to a stubborn pharaoh again and again with the same demand, "Let my people go!" And Jesus followed through on the plan of salvation though it cost Him His own life.

Courage is
being scared
to death, but
saddling up
anyway.

JOHN WAYNE, ACTOR

I AM

"Whom are you seeking?" They answered Him, "Jesus of Nazareth." Jesus said to them, "I am He."

JOHN 18:4-5 NKJV

In the Garden in Gethsemane, Judas, the disciple who betrayed Jesus, arrived with a Roman detachment of soldiers, a large number of temple guards, and officers from the chief priests and Pharisees to arrest Him. When Jesus said, "I am He," the men staggered and stumbled backward. Why did these men fall down flat? Because they found themselves in the presence of God. They had come to collect a mere man and they found the Son of God, who revealed His divine nature and glory when He uttered those three little words that carried infinite meaning.

There is power in the name of Jesus! Which is why Jesus Himself taught us how to pray in Matthew 13:2 NLT, "Whatever you ask in my name, this I will do, that the Father may be glorified in the Son." When we pray, we should always ask in the name of Jesus.

FAITH CHECK

Life began in the Garden of Eden, where sin was born, but eternal life began in the Garden of Gethsemane, the garden of suffering for Jesus, who agonized over what was to come, yet out of love for us offered His body on the cross.

The Bible is the story of two gardens, Eden and Gethsemane. In the first, Adam took a fall. In the second, Jesus took a stand.

MAX LUCADO

DREAM ON

That person is like a tree planted by streams of water,
which yields its fruit in season and whose leaf
does not wither—whatever they do prospers.

PSALM 1:3 NIV

Most of us have dreams—like opening a cozy bed-and-breakfast, inventing something amazing, starting our own company, becoming a movie star or recording artist, writing a book, being a professional athlete, or climbing Mt. Everest. It's a sad truth, but many people give up on their dreams early on because they believe that achieving them is impossible. They allow themselves to be pushed by their problems instead of being led by their dreams. Other people refuse to work toward achieving their goals and instead expect success to simply drop into their laps. Famed author and motivational speaker Zig Ziglar once said, "Success occurs when our dreams get bigger than our excuses."

FAITH CHECK

God knows the desires of your heart, and He will help you to prosper and succeed, but you have to work hard at your goals, and work even harder at trusting Him. If you get tired of waiting on God and aim for success your own way, you will settle for far less than God's best for you.

Our dreams are too small for God. His dreams are limitless. If anyone ever tells you your dreams are silly, remember there's some millionaire walking around who invented the pool noodle.

ALL THESE THINGS

But seek ye first the kingdom of God, and His righteousness;
and all these things shall be added unto you.

MATTHEW 6:33 KJV

When God came to Solomon in a dream and asked him what he wanted, Solomon could have asked for riches, or wealth, or honor, or the life of his enemies, or long life for himself (II Chronicles 1:7–11). But instead of asking for worldly things, King Solomon asked God for wisdom and knowledge to help him rule his people. Solomon's request pleased God, so the Father not only gave King Solomon what he asked for, He gave him everything else as well. Solomon's kingdom was unrivaled in the ancient world, and Solomon the man bore the fruit of every type of excellence. Which is what captivated the Queen of Sheba, who traveled over fifteen hundred miles to see for herself this wise man of God she had heard so much about.

FAITH CHECK

There is a King greater than Solomon who was born into this world. Jesus Christ, the King of all kings, who gave His life for us to inherit eternal life. The Queen of Sheba came from the uttermost parts of the earth just to hear the wisdom of an earthly king, yet the only distance we have to travel to meet God Himself is from our knees to the floor.

When life
gets too hard
to stand, kneel.

BABBLING

*Come, let us build ourselves a city, with a tower that reaches
to the heavens, so that we may make a name for ourselves.*

GENESIS 11:4 NIV

The people of the earth, descendants of Noah after the flood, once shared one common language. They decided to settle together in Shinar, later called Babylon. There, they began to build a magnificent tower to the heavens so they could be like gods themselves, instead of worshipping *the* God who created them. But God saw what they were up to and "kerfuzzled" the people of Babel with new languages so they couldn't understand one another, and He scattered them over the earth. The word *babble* comes from this event and means "to talk fast and continuously in an incomprehensible way."

There are many towers like Babel today—towers of pride, arrogance, and rebellion. But one day the confusion of Babel will be done away with and there will be no more worship of idols and false gods. Believers will again speak one language, the pure language of heaven (Zephaniah 3:9), and will worship together, singing God's praises in fellowship.

FAITH CHECK

For those who live in humility, repentance, and faith, there is only one tower to turn to. "For thou hast been a shelter for me, and a strong tower from the enemy" (Psalm 61:3 KJV).

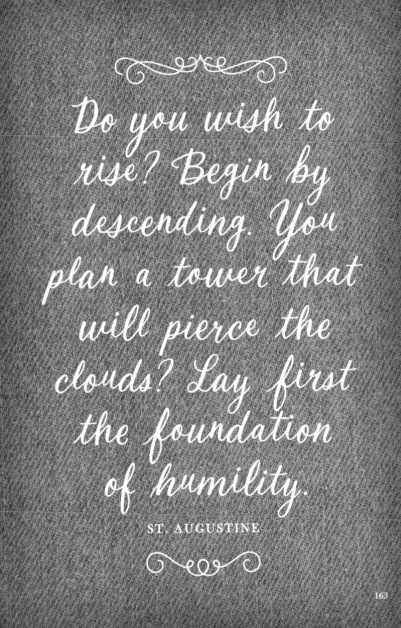

Do you wish to rise? Begin by descending. You plan a tower that will pierce the clouds? Lay first the foundation of humility.

ST. AUGUSTINE

163

CAFETERIA

*For the time will come when people
will not put up with sound doctrine.*

II TIMOTHY 4:3 NIV

Most of us have been to a cafeteria-style restaurant at least once in our lives. The places are all different, but the set-ups are basically the same. You grab a tray, place it on a little ledge, and slide that tray along while your tummy rumbles at the sight of all the delicious foods displayed behind glass cases: fried chicken, fish planks, meat loaf, roast beef, mashed potatoes, macaroni and cheese, perfect Parker house rolls glistening with butter, petite bowls of wiggling, jiggling gelatin, and an assortment of perfect pies and other tantalizing desserts at the end. Some of us like cafeterias so much we apply the same method to our faith, choosing the side dishes and desserts while ignoring the meat and potatoes. There are people who deny miracles in the Bible, calling them "fanciful myths." Others consider the entire Bible to be metaphorical. Still others choose to see God's commands more as suggestions, but they want God to bless them without any personal accountability. A person can disagree with the Bible, but God is completely righteous. A side order of this and a side order of that will not make a person right with God.

FAITH CHECK

The meat and potatoes of the Christian faith is the death, burial, and resurrection of Jesus Christ our Savior. "That if you confess with your mouth the Lord Jesus and believe in your heart that God raised Him from the dead, you will be saved" (Romans 10:9 NKJV).

God owes
us nothing
but gives us
everything.

THE CHURCH WITH
THE GOLDEN HAND

*The fruit of the righteous is a tree of life,
and he who wins souls is wise*

PROVERBS 11:30 NKJV

Completed in 1860, the First Presbyterian Church of Port Gibson's most noticeable feature sits atop its magnificent steeple—a golden eleven-foot-tall metal hand, the index finger pointing upwards toward heaven. The church's pastor, Reverend Zebulon Butler, faithfully served his congregation for over three decades. He was known for his fire-and-brimstone sermons, which he often accentuated by jabbing his index finger upwards towards heaven, like a quivering compass needle. For years prior to the Civil War, he encouraged his congregation to build the new church, but sadly, he died on the eve of its unveiling. In fact, the first service in the new sanctuary was his own memorial service. The congregation decided to honor their beloved pastor with a symbol of his well-remembered gesture, a fitting tribute to Reverend Butler, who served his congregation and his God with all his heart.

FAITH CHECK

The calling of every believer is to be a pointer, to offer directions to those who are lost, that the way to heaven is through a door whose name is Jesus.

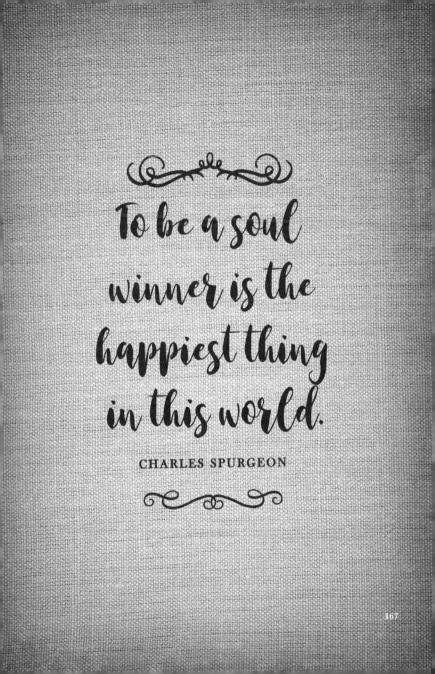

To be a soul
winner is the
happiest thing
in this world.

CHARLES SPURGEON

THE GRANDFATHER CLOCK

So teach us to number our days,
that we may apply our hearts unto wisdom

PSALM 90:12 KJV

O ver one hundred years ago, there were two bachelor brothers who managed a small hotel in England. In the hotel lobby was a floor clock that kept extraordinarily good time. When one of the brothers died suddenly, the old clock started to lose time. Clock smiths were summoned to repair the clock, but they were not able to fix it. The aged timepiece first lost fifteen minutes a day, then an hour. The old clock stopped working altogether when the surviving brother passed away at the age of ninety. An American songwriter, Henry Clay Work, happened to stay at the hotel many years later. When he heard the tale, he was inspired to compose a song about the clock: "It was bought on the morn of the day that he was born, and was always his treasure and pride; but it stopped short, never to go again when the old man died." "My Grandfather's Clock" became a wildly popular song, and from that point on, floor clocks were referred to as grandfather clocks.

FAITH CHECK

God determines the number of our days on this earth, and only He knows how long we will live. We will not live a second longer or die a second earlier (Job 14:5). And when our time ends on the earth, the countdown on our lives will cease, and we will no longer be bound by earthly timepieces.

Even a broken
clock is right
twice a day.

VENTURE NOT

Don't team up with those who are unbelievers.
How can righteousness be a partner with wickedness?
How can light live with darkness?

II CORINTHIANS 6:14 NLT

Have you ever felt obligated to partner up with someone when you know you shouldn't? Jehoshaphat, king of Judah, was allied by marriage with King Ahab of Israel, who asked the king to join him in battle. Jehoshaphat asked Ahab to inquire of God's prophets first. He wanted to know that God would be on their side in the battle. However, Ahab only surrounded himself with "yes men" who told him what he wanted to hear. All except one—Micaiah, who told Ahab God's true word, that he would lose the battle. Though Jehoshaphat had his doubts about Ahab, he was an honorable man and went out to fight anyway. But Ahab pulled a fast one. He decided to go to battle in disguise yet urged Jehoshaphat to wear his royal robes, which made King Jehoshaphat a sitting duck! King Jehoshaphat cried out to God, however, and the Lord provided a way of escape. King Ahab did not fare so well. An arrow struck him in between the plates of his armor and he died.

FAITH CHECK

Upon his safe return home, King Jehoshaphat heard from the prophet Jehu, who asked, "Should you help the wicked and love those who hate the LORD?" (II Chronicles 19:2 NKJV). When we partner with the ungodly, we are fighting against the God we serve.

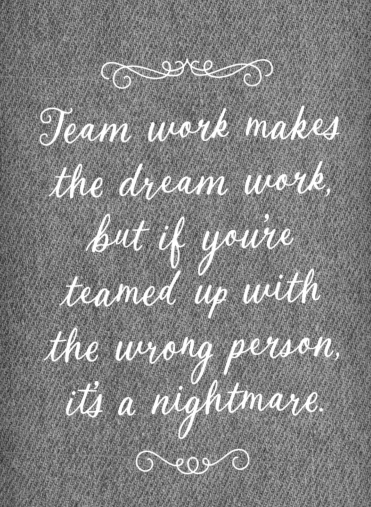

Team work makes the dream work, but if you're teamed up with the wrong person, it's a nightmare.

THE BIRD GIRL

I have seen something else under the sun: The race is not to the swift or the battle to the strong, nor does food come to the wise or wealth to the brilliant or favor to the learned; but time and chance happen to them all

ECCLESIASTES 9:11 NIV

Tucked away in Savannah, Georgia's historic Bonaventure Cemetery, an obscure sculpture of a little girl with her arms extended adorned a family plot. A photographer, commissioned to take a photograph for a book cover, happened to spot the combination statue/birdseed feeder in the dusk of an early evening. The hauntingly beautiful photograph wound up on the cover of a best-selling novel, also figuring prominently in a later film version. From that point on, fans beat a path to the cemetery to see the statue, marveling at its pure and serene simplicity. However, due to its unexpected popularity, the *Bird Girl* statue had to be permanently relocated to an art museum. One question begs to be asked: if the photographer had taken a photograph of some other statue in the Bonaventure Cemetery that evening, would a different sculpture have inspired such fervor? Fame seems to follow no formula or reason, yet it finds those to whom it is given.

FAITH CHECK

In this world, one might be famous, or infamous, but earthly fame in either form is fleeting. But did you know that God has His own hall of fame? His "Faith Hall of Fame" is an impressive list of Old Testament heroes of the Bible in Hebrews 11—ordinary men and women who triumphed over adversity and whose stories both encourage and challenge our faith.

The desire for
fame tempts
even noble
minds.

ST. AUGUSTINE

WEEDS

The weeds are the sons of the evil one, and the enemy who sowed them is the devil. The harvest is the end of the age, and the reapers are angels. Just as the weeds are gathered and burned with fire, so will it be at the end of the age.

MATTHEW 13:38-40 ESV

Anyone who has a garden experiences the aggravation of undesirable plants. Weeds grow where other plants grow, but they also grow where other plants won't. They spring up overnight and are so hardy that if a portion of root is left behind after it is plucked, the weed will pop back up days later.

Imagine that your heart is like a garden, a valuable piece of acreage to the Lord. Out of it can come an abundance of good fruit to His kingdom. But when we allow weeds to invade the garden of our heart, they multiply and choke out the fruitful plants, replacing them with unfruitful thorns and thistles. What are the weeds of this world? Desires, distractions, and fears—all idols to self-interest. We cultivate the soil of our hearts by tending to the things of God and plucking up what doesn't belong.

FAITH CHECK

The phrase "God's Acre" is a name for a churchyard or burial ground and comes from a German word meaning "field of God." Those who die in Christ are buried, like seeds in the earth, and will one day rise and live again at the Second Coming of Jesus Christ.

Weed it
and reap.

THEY CALL THEMSELVES CHRISTIANS

If we endure, we will also reign with Him.
If we deny Him, He also will deny us.
II TIMOTHY 2:12 NKJV

Soldiers in the Roman army identified themselves with their generals by adding the suffix *-ian* at the end of the general's name. Therefore, a Caesarian soldier would be a solider serving under Caesar. In Latin, the word *ian* means "the party of." In the early church in Antioch, people began to call followers of Christ Christians, though the use of the name was likely said at first in the spirit of mockery. However, the name stuck and soon believers also began to call themselves Christians, happily adding the suffix to the end of Christ's to indicate that they were with Jesus. Early Christians joyfully sent a message to the world that they were followers of Christ, though the message cost many of them their lives. A believer's life begins at the altar where we surrender our nothing for everything, and sometimes ends on another altar, where believers are forced to decide whether to sacrifice everything for nothing. "Choose you this day whom ye will serve." (Joshua 24:15 KJV).

FAITH CHECK

If you knew that openly announcing to the world that you are a Christian would cost you your job, your standing in the community, or your very life, would you call yourself a Christian?

No wound?
No scar? Yet as
the Master shall
the servant be, and
pierced are the feet
that follow Me.

AMY CARMICHAEL

HAPPY LITTLE TREES

*You keep him in perfect peace whose mind is
stayed on you, because he trusts in you*
ISAIAH 26:3 ESV

Bob Ross was a popular American painter, art instructor, and television host who created a show called *The Joy of Painting* that aired from 1983 to 1994 on PBS. He was as popular for his painting techniques as he was for his calm, laid back personality, and for his impossibly poufy, permed 'fro. People responded positively to his casual and simple approach to painting. He was fond of telling beginner artists who felt that they had messed up their canvas, "We don't make mistakes, we have happy accidents."

Most of us are so afraid of failing that we give up before we truly get started. But instead of giving up, why not give yourself permission to make mistakes? Apply what you learn from those mistakes, and then try again.

FAITH CHECK

Bob Ross took the performance anxiety and stress out of painting and transformed it into an enjoyable and relaxing pastime for many people. He wasn't a Michelangelo, but he was a hundred percent himself. Ross's cheerful, optimistic outlook on life influenced and encouraged many people to explore their artistic side without pressure or judgment. We could all use some encouragement and optimism in our lives. "Therefore encourage one another and build one other up, just as you are doing" (I Thessalonians 5:11 ESV).

In painting, you have unlimited power. You have the ability to move mountains. You can bend rivers. But when I get home, the only thing I have power over is the garbage.

ARTIST BOB ROSS

Adam and Eve

*Now the serpent was more cunning than any beast of the field
which the LORD God had made. And he said to the woman,
"Has God indeed said, 'You shall not eat of every tree of the garden'?"*

GENESIS 3:1 NKJV

A century ago, medicine men would travel in wagons from town to town selling cures in a bottle. Their products, so-called snake oil, were heralded as panaceas for every ailment known to mankind. People not only bought the bottle, they bought the lie. The salesmen's claims, however, were fraudulent, and their concoctions were not only dangerous but sometimes deadly.

Satan's been selling us his own brand of snake oil from the beginning, and it's still just as dangerous and deadly to mankind. He sold Adam and Eve the lie that God was withholding something good from them. Back then, although they lacked for nothing, Adam and Eve thought they needed the fruit of the Tree of the Knowledge of Good and Evil. They fell for the lie. Nowadays, we chase after every ungodly thing we desire and every low-hanging fruit, but nothing we gain is ever enough to satisfy us. We buy Satan's lie that God wants us to have everything that pleases us, even if those desires are outside of God's will.

FAITH CHECK

There is only one cure to our ailment, and it is found on a very different tree, a cross of rough-hewn wood where Jesus stretched out His arms and died for us, that we might have life eternal with God.

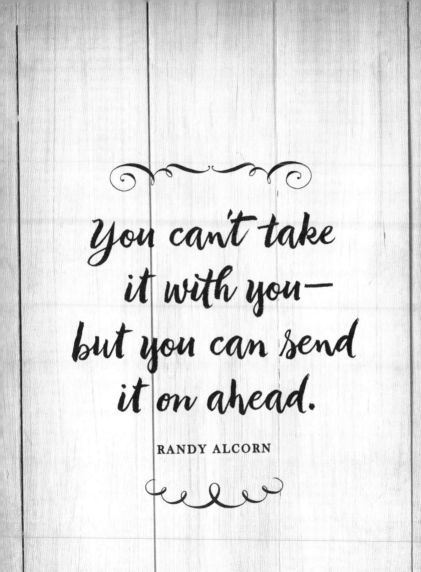

You can't take
it with you—
but you can send
it on ahead.

RANDY ALCORN

TO GOD ALONE

*For all that is in the world—the desires of the flesh
and the desires of the eyes and the pride of life—
is not from the Father but is from the world.*

I JOHN 2:16 ESV

Pride is the downfall of many an individual, especially those who have been gifted with extraordinary talents or abilities. The temptation to glory in oneself and one's accomplishments is almost too strong to avoid. However, there are two sure ways of avoiding self-adulation. One way is to give God the glory for everything. One of the most famous composers of all time, Johann Sebastian Bach, wrote the initials S.D.G. at the end of all his church compositions. Translated from Latin, *Soli Deo Gloria*, the initials mean "Glory to God Alone." Though he was unquestionably a musical genius, Bach wasn't interested in fame or fortune.

The second way to avoid becoming prideful is to serve others with a humble heart. Bach was a famous composer but he also taught music to many students. He once told a young student who felt discouraged, "Just practice diligently, and it will go very well. You have five fingers on each hand just as healthy as mine."

FAITH CHECK

Bach believed that music was a blessing from God and that music should be used to glorify God and to edify men and women on the earth. Like Bach, instead of allowing yourself or your work to become the focus of anyone's adoration, turn all the attention back to God, who gave you the gift in the first place.

A proud man is always looking down on things and people; and, of course, as long as you are looking down, you cannot see something that is above you.

C. S. LEWIS.

SANDCASTLES

A wise man. . . built his house on the rock.
MATTHEW 7:24 NIV

Sandcastles are the most beautiful and ephemeral sights to enjoy on any beach. One cannot fail to marvel at the whimsical turrets and towers, spindles, moats, and drawbridges rising from the buff sheen of wave-wet sand. To build a sandcastle requires buckets and molds, shovels and other tools. The formula for building a sandcastle is one part sand to one part water, plus an entire day of hard work in the hot sun. Once completed, a charming castle-in-the-sand will draw onlookers and admirers with approval and compliments for the architect. But the builder will not take pride in his work for long. The natural world has a way of humbling our creations. Soon the high tide will come in and the castle will crumble with each rolling wave until there is no sign that the beautiful creation ever existed. Sandcastles were never meant to last, only to be appreciated in the short time they exist.

FAITH CHECK

In the scheme of eternity, our lives on this earth exist no longer than a sandcastle lasts on the beach. When we build our hopes and dreams on shifting sand, they will one day be washed away, and all that we lived for and accomplished will also be forgotten. But mold your character, pour on living water, and build your life on Jesus Christ and His righteousness, and the new creation you are will not crumble but stand forever in God's kingdom.

On Christ, the
solid Rock, I stand;
all other ground
is sinking sand.

EDWARD MOTE

MANY RUSHING WATERS

Then I heard what sounded like a great multitude, like
the roar of rushing waters and like loud peals of thunder,
shouting: "Hallelujah! For our Lord God Almighty reigns.

REVELATION 19:6 NIV

Every second, 3,160 tons of water flow over Niagara Falls, the collective name for three waterfalls that straddle the border between Canada and the United States. On a calm morning, some claim to be able to discern the distant thunder of the Falls eighteen or more miles away. But as one draws closer, ten miles nearer, then five miles, one mile—the boom of the rushing water becomes louder. Finally, when one is standing at the railing that overlooks the magnificent Falls, it is impossible to hear anything but the thunderous tumult of water—a majestic deluge of cascading waters.

God's voice is like the sound of many waters, of many rivers falling together, and He will make Himself heard to those who are both near and far. The closer you draw near to God, the closer He will draw near to you, and the easier it will be to hear Him (James 4:8). And His voice, like the sound of many waters, will drown out all the other voices of this world calling for your attention.

FAITH CHECK

Everyone wants to hear from God. We all need direction. Answers. Reassurance. But how can we understand what He is saying? God spoke to the Old Testament prophets in a variety of ways. And God speaks to us as well—through His Word, and sometimes in the still, small voice of the Holy Spirit.

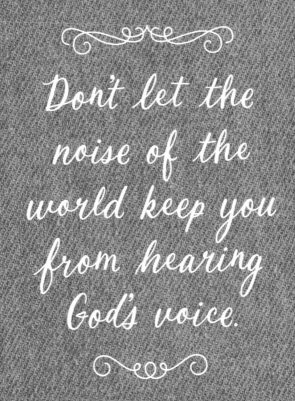

Don't let the noise of the world keep you from hearing God's voice.

COMPASS

The LORD directs the steps of the godly.
He delights in every detail of their lives.

PSALM 37:23 NLT

Every good scout has a compass, but how do they work? Magnetic compasses have a magnetized needle that aligns itself with the earth's magnetic field and points to the "magnetic north." Some scientists believe that lodestones, mostly found on the earth's surface, are magnetized by the strong magnetic fields surrounding lightning bolts that strike the ground. "He covers His hands with the lightning and commands it to strike the mark" (Job 36:32 ESV). Imagine that: God loves us so much He provided small rocks imbued with power to help us find our way around the earth! And His love for us is greater still, because He sent His only Son, Jesus Christ, the Rock of our salvation, and imbued Him with all power and authority to show us the way to eternal life.

FAITH CHECK

A compass is an instrument used for navigation, to discern which direction to follow in order to reach our destination here on earth. God's Word, the Bible, is our "Christ Compass" to show us the way. But unlike a regular compass, in order to discern which direction to go, we must align ourselves with the truth in order to reach our heavenly destination.

The Bible
is a compass
for the soul.

LIVE YOUR FAITH

Dear Friend,

This book was prayerfully crafted with you, the reader, in mind—every word, every sentence, every page—was thoughtfully written, designed, and packaged to encourage you...right where you are this very moment. At DaySpring, our vision is to see every person experience the life-changing message of God's love. So, as we worked through rough drafts, design changes, edits and details, we prayed for you to deeply experience His unfailing love, indescribable peace, and pure joy. It is our sincere hope that through these Truth-filled pages your heart will be blessed, knowing that God cares about you—your desires and disappointments, your challenges and dreams.

He knows. He cares. He loves you unconditionally.

BLESSINGS!
THE DAYSPRING BOOK TEAM

....

**Additional copies of this book and
other DaySpring titles can be purchased
at fine bookstores everywhere.
Order online at dayspring.com
or
by phone at 1-877-751-4347**

DaySpring

Dear Friend,

This book was prayerfully crafted with you, the reader, in mind—every word, every sentence, every page—was thoughtfully written, designed, and packaged to encourage you...right where you are this very moment. At DaySpring, our vision is to see every person experience the life-changing message of God's love. So, as we worked through rough drafts, design changes, edits and details, we prayed for you to deeply experience His unfailing love, indescribable peace, and pure joy. It is our sincere hope that through these Truth-filled pages your heart will be blessed, knowing that God cares about you—your desires and disappointments, your challenges and dreams.

He knows. He cares. He loves you unconditionally.

BLESSINGS!
THE DAYSPRING BOOK TEAM

Additional copies of this book and
other DaySpring titles can be purchased
at fine bookstores everywhere.
Order online at dayspring.com
or
by phone at 1-877-751-4347